Walking Calcutta

by

Keith Humphrey

**Grosvenor House
Publishing Limited**

This book is published by
Grosvenor House Publishing Ltd
28-30 High Street, Guildford, Surrey, GU1 3HY.
www.grosvenorhousepublishing.co.uk

A CIP record for this book
is available from the British Library

ISBN 978-1-907211-04-1

WALKING CALCUTTA

On foot around Central and North Calcutta
by Keith Humphrey

To the people of Calcutta
The unsung eighth wonder of the world
for their many kindnesses to me

There are others who must shoulder their share
of the blame for this work.
Principal amongst these is Sugato Dutt, gentleman of
Calcutta, who foolishly encouraged me in this enterprise

About the Author

The author, a veteran traveller of the Indian sub-continent, has a love and fascination for Calcutta and its people undiminished since his first encounter with the City nearly four decades ago.

On his extensive travels he is invariably accompanied by his favourite travelling companion, his wife. Together they have a grown up daughter and, when in England, live by the sea on the Suffolk coast.

Contents

CONTENTS

Street Maps

I am grateful to D.P. Publications and Sales Concern of
66 College Street, Calcutta
for their kind consent in allowing me to reproduce the
street maps which appear in this work and of which they
hold copyright

None of these street maps are drawn to scale.

Ward boundaries are denoted by a narrow broken line;
the route of the Metro Railway by a thick broken line

I am also indebted to Chris Smy for his enhancement
and artwork to the street map and cover images

'If you have one Calcuttan, you have a poet
If you have two you have a political party
If you have three you have two political parties'

(Indian adage)

(Author's note)

In January 2001, Calcutta officially renamed itself Kolkata, which is more in line with the Bengali pronunciation. In this work I have exclusively used 'Calcutta,' not in any attitude of wilful defiance but simply because it seems more appropriate given the many historical references I have made concerning the City.

Introduction

There will be few travellers from the west conditioned to meet with equanimity their first encounter with Calcutta; they will be even less equipped to do so if it is also to be their first experience of India. They will have come in some trepidation to a City about which they have heard fearful accounts; where hearsay and rumour suggests exists an urban awfulness of an unimaginable scale and where the destitute and leprous lay dying in the gutters around every street corner. They would do well to forget all of this and come with an open mind; there will be time enough to form a view from their own firsthand experience of the City.

Amongst even seasoned and experienced travellers from the west, the name Calcutta, is for some, synonymous with rumours of dreadful poverty, of tides of refugees, famine, disease, political unrest and riot and some of the most appalling urban habitation conditions on earth. There is some truth in all of this; Calcutta has experienced all of these things, although not necessarily at the same time, to the degree often supposed or even within living memory.

It has been Calcutta's misfortune that the City has become a kind of metaphor for everything that popularly represents the urban hell-hole of apocalyptic imagination. It seems nearly always to have been the negative, and so rarely the positive that has been most frequently accentuated in connection with Calcutta. Few commentators, unless they were locals, have ever said anything nice about Calcutta and many have been downright uncomplimentary about the place. This has done much to prejudice the expectations of first time travellers to the City and to colour the image held by the many who will never travel there. Many, though by no means all, of the most damning indictments which have been made against Calcutta are reflections or exaggerations on conditions existing in the 1960's and 1970's when it really did look like the City was in danger of imploding under the huge strains being placed upon it, not least from the massive influx of both economic migrants from neighbouring States and refugees fleeing the turmoil which gave birth to the neighbouring nation of Bangladesh.

The last three decades or so have proved the more dire predictions wrong: Calcutta did not implode but moved on. Today it is a noticeably different City than that I first visited nearly forty years ago. Calcutta remains one of the great cities of the world notwithstanding that very real problems still exist there. A balance needs to be struck: it is misleading and unfair to equate Calcutta with the sort of conditions described as existing in the fictitious 'Anand Nager' slum of La Pierre's novel 'City of Joy' (which in any event was located in Howrah not Calcutta), or in the leper colonies and squatter encampments out near the dumping grounds of Dhapa. There are many other positive and inspiring aspects to Calcutta which are all too often overlooked by the traveller from the west or, as is more likely, never seen at all.

One of the main barriers to a better understanding of Calcutta is that so few western travellers seem to spend very long there; two to four days seems to be the norm. In their stay, most will confine themselves to the central environs of Chowringhee, (or Jawaharlal Nehru Road as stretches of that fine thoroughfare are now known); the hotels of Sudder Street, Lindsay Street and in and around Shakespeare Sarani being popular destinations. The nearby Victoria Memorial, Indian Museum, Maidan, the old Writers' Building, Job Charnock's Mausoleum and the shops of the affluent end of Park Street provide convenient sightseeing. The more adventurous may head north to cross the iconic Howrah Bridge spanning the River Hooghly; view the idiosyncratic collections of the Mullick family, housed in the Marble Palace, located off Chitteranjan Avenue or browse amongst the book stalls in College Street. A few may head East down Park Street to the old British Cemetery or along the Circular Road to visit the late Mother Theresa's house and the head house of The Missionaries of Charity, the order she founded. Otherwise, it will be rare indeed to find a western traveller on foot anywhere to the north or east of Dalhousie Square; areas which contain some of the oldest, most interesting and the least documented quarters of the City.

This work is built around a series of suggested walking tours through different areas and to various destinations in central and north Calcutta. I have concentrated on these particular areas not only because of their historical and social interest, which is considerable, but also because most, having been largely ignored by travel writers, will be virtually unknown to travellers from the west.

Many of these areas are criss-crossed by a bewildering maze of small lanes or gullees. This, in part, is what can give such interest to exploring Calcutta on foot. Full directions are given for each of the suggested walks and a set of sketch maps included at the end of each chapter. Every walk can be completed comfortably and at a leisurely pace, in under half a day. A decent basic compass and a notebook will prove useful together with a good supply of water, essential in the summer months.

For me Calcutta has always been a very special place; indeed I believe there to be no other place on earth quite like it. If this small work can encourage the traveller to see and experience Calcutta in a way they otherwise would have missed, then it will have achieved its purpose.

3

Foreword

On being a Pedestrian in Calcutta:

You can achieve a better understanding of any city if you are prepared to walk its highways and byways. You travel more slowly so have better opportunity to see far more, of both the good and the bad, than you will ever gather from the back seat of a taxi or tourist mini-bus. More importantly is that in walking you move in closer proximity with the city's populace; they are more accessible to you, as you are to them. Nowhere can this be more rewarding than in teeming Calcutta.

Walking for pleasure and as the preferred means of exploration, particularly in the hotter, more humid seasons, does not score highly in the list of desirable pastimes of the average citizen of Calcutta. As a consequence, you often find yourself the subject of these good people's polite curiosity. Once they have established that you do not have a driver waiting around the corner and that you will be walking everywhere during your stay in their City, I have frequently detected more than a hint of surprise, sometimes approaching mild alarm, at this, to them, clear eccentricity of behaviour.

The main considerations for the pedestrian in Calcutta are climate, traffic and what lies underfoot; not necessarily in that order.

The climate of Calcutta, situated as it is on what was once swampland and salt marsh astride the Tropic of Cancer can

5

provide a punishing environment. The winter months, from October to February provide weather that is mainly dry and 'relatively' cool, although to the latter end temperatures often rise to 33C/36C. The summer months, from March to May are seriously hot with temperatures rarely below 36C and often as high as 42C. Added to this heat is the humidity. It is quite common for this to stick at 98/99% for weeks on end. The summer months are followed by the monsoon, generally from June to September. During these months there will be times when many streets in central and north Calcutta are awash with rainwater; where motor traffic and trams cannot move, only the hardy rickshaw pullers who are then the kings of the road.

Traffic considerations for the pedestrian in Calcutta are twofold. Pollution levels from traffic are very high and seemingly ever present. There is just no avoiding it. The second issue is the aggressiveness of Calcutta's traffic: second only to that found in lawless Patna, in the nearby State of Bihar. There is a clear hierarchy based on size with heavy lorries, buses and trams at the top and you, the vulnerable pedestrian, at the bottom; below even, the long suffering rickshaw puller. Never assume traffic will give way to you when crossing a road; it will not. In the main thoroughfares, use only the controlled crossings (often manned by the excellent, white uniformed, Calcutta Traffic Police). If in any doubt, follow the locals who have, of necessity, developed highly tuned survival instincts. Be particularly wary of the passenger buses operated by private undertakings. These will stop suddenly, almost anywhere, to set down and pick up passengers. They will move off with as little warning, or care and their drivers are notorious, for being speed crazed, risk takers. You will read almost daily, reports in the City's press of accidents, often with fatalities, involving these vehicles. Such reports generally conclude with a comment to the effect that the driver and conductor absconded: a wise move given the anger often evoked in passengers and pedestrians by such incidents.

With few exceptions, the footpaths of Calcutta's thoroughfares are challenging to the pedestrian. In the main roads throughout the City there can be hardly ten consecutive metres of unobstructed or reasonably flat pavement on which to tread. You and fellow pedestrians will have to share the pavement with small traders, astrologers, catering enterprises, chai stalls, sleepers, badly parked vehicles, goats, chickens, dogs, bathers at standpipes, ramshackle temporary settlements, madly placed lighting columns and advertising hoardings and the ever present but unexplained piles of rubble. All life is here, it is relentless, inescapable and a privilege to be amongst it all.

One further peculiarity of Calcutta is that almost every pavement appears to have been repeatedly excavated to lay or repair the service pipes and cables beneath but never properly reinstated. The result is that the excavations have either been underfilled, providing a kind of zigzag, gully, often rain filled, or overfilled, creating a sort of meandering hump which, try as you might, you can never quite, successfully keep both feet either side of.

On Street Names and Numbering

To the uninitiated, the naming of Calcutta's streets and the numbering of the buildings within them can be confusing, amusing and sometimes mildly frustrating

Over a number of years, the Calcutta Municipal Corporation has engaged in the renaming of literally hundreds of the City's thoroughfares. It even has a standing Road Renaming Committee for this purpose. Often, the motive for renaming has been to introduce an Indian and remove an Imperial connection. Hence, Cornwallis Street became Bidhan Sarani, Amherst Street, Raja Ram Mohan Road, Charnock Place Netaji Subhas Road, Harrison Road Mahatma Ghandi Road and so on. Interestingly, there have been some splendid omissions. Still lurking just south of Shakespeare Sarani are some thoroughfares of blatantly imperialist connection, these being Victoria Terrace and Albert Road, each occupying a side of Victoria Square. In other cases, street names have been changed to honour respected and significant Indian and other personalities. For example, Chitpore Road became Rabindra Sarani, the Lower Circular Road A.J. Chandra Bose Road, Dharmatala Street Lenin Sarani and so on.

Sometimes these new names have caught on, sometimes they have not. Not all such renaming seems to have met with majority approval by the City's citizens. The result is that often you will find both the old and the new names in common usage, depending on who you are talking to or which map, guide or reference book you consult. For example, Dalhousie Square seems more widely used than the new name B.B.D. Bagh. Likewise, Chowringhee seems to enjoy wider usage than Jawaharlal Nehru Road as does Sealdah Fly Over than Bidyapati Setu or Canning Street over Biplabi Rash Behari Bose Road. There are scores of similar examples of this dual usage, all seemingly designed to confound the traveller intent on exploring Calcutta.

Where the Corporation's Road Renaming Committee has really excelled itself is where it has renamed only part of a continuous thoroughfare or has allocated different names to different stretches. Beadon Street, travelling west to east, is first Beadon Street, then Dani Ghosh Sarani, then back to Beadon Street and, finally, Abhedananda Road. It is much the same with Colotolla Street which becomes Maulana Saukat Ali Lane as it nears Chitteranjan Avenue and, east of this, Anagarika Dharmapala Street.

To help overcome potential confusion, a list of the old street names and their replacement new names is included at Annexe 3 to this work. This list is by no means exhaustive, being mainly

8

restricted to the thoroughfares of those quarters of the City to which the suggested walking tours relate.

The provision of formal street nameplates in Calcutta can also be patchy. The older quarters of the City are the best signed but be prepared for the sign to read the old, rather than the new street name or to be spelt in an archaic form.

Of enormous help to navigation is that nearly every shop or business, however small, includes the address on their sign-board. Again, be prepared for inconsistencies. It is not at all uncommon to find adjoining premises where one will display the new street name and the other the old name. Equally helpful, particularly outside of commercial areas, is the widespread use of mail boxes affixed to most residential premises. These invariably show the family name, house number and street name. Incredibly, these sometimes show both the old and new street names. Hence, the mail box of the thoughtful Ghose family of Amar Bose Sarani reminds passersby that this thoroughfare was once called, and is still known by many, as Chor Bagan Lane.

Street numbering enjoys particular peculiarities for the traveller to grasp. First amongst these is that a street number can relate to the whole block in which a particular premises is situated. The block itself may contain very many individual premises which, to outward appearance all seem separate entities. So, when at first you are unable to find any trace of, say Dutt Travel Ltd at 207 Rabindra Sarani, the chances are that it is located down the adjoining side street which forms part of the same block which faces Rabindra Sarani. It will share the 207 Rabindra Sarani address, proudly displayed on the shop front name board but actually the premises is physically located half way down adjoining Burtolla Street.

Another difficulty is where there has been demolition which has fragmented once single continuous thoroughfares. This is often found where the old Calcutta Improvement Trust (CIT) had been active. A good example can be found in what remains of Calcutta's old Chinatown to the North of B.B Ganguly Street between the Rabindra Sarani and Chitteranjan Avenue crossings. Here, you will find the ancient Blackburn Lane now scattered in three separate locations, following division by demolition and the laying out of India Exchange Place Extension and New C.I.T. Road. Here, as in other similarly affected locations, no renumbering seems to have taken place to compensate for the buildings cleared away.

On Personal Space and Privacy

From the moment the western traveller first sets foot in Calcutta all previously held concepts of privacy and personal space must be abandoned. For the traveller has come to one of the most densely populated cities on earth and, until departure, will have hardly a waking moment when not part of a crowd or more than half an arm's length away from a fellow human being. To illustrate this, the latest (2001) census data gives a population density per square kilometre of the area covered by the Calcutta Municipal Corporation, of 24,760. This is an average figure; within some wards in the central and northern parts of the City, Muchipara for example, the density will be higher, in some cases up to 31,500. By comparison the corresponding figures for New York and for London are 10,452 and 4,697 respectively. Even teeming Bombay (Mumbai), now the most populous city on the sub-continent, is less densely populated than Calcutta, with a corresponding figure of 22,658.

Staggering though these figures are, there is more to it than mere numbers suggest. So much of life in Calcutta takes place on the streets, where you can have your hair cut, be shaved, have your fortune told, your washing, ironing and cooking done, eat, bathe and sleep if you wish to, that the notion of personal space sinks to irrelevance. You are perhaps only reminded of the notion when walking across the Maidan, possibly the only truly open space anywhere in Calcutta proper where you could confidently hurl a chapatti in any direction without fear of hitting someone. Even on those very rare occasions when you may believe yourself to be alone, you seldom are in fact. There will be any number of times when, on sitting to take a rest in some relatively quiet backwater, you hear a disembodied 'hello' cast in your direction. It may take you some minutes to discover the source of this greeting, often found to be an open window, doorway or a balcony above where your unseen company has been loitering. If there is any corner of Calcutta where it is possible to be truly alone, then I have yet to find it.

Then there is the business of nosiness. Indians because they are one of the most intelligent peoples on earth are also amongst the most curious and nowhere is this trait more pronounced than in Calcutta. There seems to be a positive virtue in knowing the business of others and of them knowing yours. The Indians are great observers who love involving themselves in your affairs, however fleetingly. You can hardly ever stop to consult a map, take a compass reading or look at something without attracting at least a few curious passers-by. I was once sat near the Srimani Market up in north Calcutta, absorbed in writing up my notes and consulting my maps. On looking up I discovered that, in the few minutes I had been sitting there, a small crowd of at least a dozen people had gathered around me, curious to see what this 'firinghee' was up to. There was even a kind of spokesman, relaying to those without such a good view, exactly what was going on. All this inquisitiveness is conducted in the most polite and friendly manner and nor is it at all one-sided. Countless times I have been passing by some incident or mild altercation which, in true Calcutta fashion, I have stopped to observe. It is nearly always the case that one of your fellow observers will feel compelled to tell you what it is all about together with any relevant background to the incident or, if known, the respective characters of the parties involved.

Until the traveller adjusts, all this observation and inquisitiveness can breed feelings of mild paranoia in the less emotionally secure. So many times it will happen that the traveller returns, seemingly unobserved, to their lodgings or hotel room when, almost immediately, there is a knock at the door. It will be your laundry, a message, a bill to sign. You saw no one on your return but 'they' knew you were back, indeed the very minute you were back. The first time my wife and I stayed at the old Great Eastern Hotel, we would return to our room in the evenings through the labyrinthine, dimly lit and deserted corridors with not a soul in sight. But the minute we turned into our corridor and long before we gained our room, two and sometimes three smiling faces would appear from the room used by housekeeping staff at the far end of the passageway. We never once succeeded in reaching our room undetected. It became a kind of elaborate game, which we never won.

Prologue

Calcutta Daybreak

To walk in the streets of Calcutta in those fitful few hours either side of sunrise can be the prelude to another and deeper understanding of what this City is about. It can be a salutary and at the same time, slightly unnerving experience but, to the observant traveller, one that is always worth the loss of an extra few hours sleep.

It is at this time that the slumbering trams and buses begin to stir; when lonely taxis move slowly in half deserted roads which are soon to pullulate with humanity like few other places on earth.

In the still darkened side streets and lanes off Chitteranjan Avenue, from Bow Bazar crossing in the South to Sovabazar crossing in the North, indistinct forms, concealed in blankets and other coverings, begin to shift position. With attendant hawking, for this is a City with many respiratory problems amongst the poor, some rise to a sitting position, some fully upright whilst others remain prone. Along the pavements in the corners of buildings, small cooking fires spring out promising the first meal of the day ahead. Beyond the Mahatma Ghandi Road crossing, lamps are lit on chai stalls where the early risers begin to gather in small groups gossiping in the polyglot tongues which are such a feature of Calcutta. Nearby, dealers in Paan, that spiced araca nut concoction wrapped in a betel leaf to be chewed and spat out to stain the pavement redly, will be trading from tiny and dimly lit cubby holes or from pavement stalls.

At this hour rickshaw pullers can move relatively unimpeded by aggressive traffic and many are already heading out to their respective stands, in search of their first fare. Others are still sitting or sleeping on their stationary rickshaws; those awake gently tapping their bells against the shafts, perhaps from habit for there are still few passers-by to attract as potential passengers.

Already, coolies (for in Calcutta this is a justifiably respectful title), are mustering at points around the Mechua Fruit Market, in Burra Bazar, Chandni Chowk, Posta and, Manicktala Markets and in and around Bow Bazar. Soon to begin that seemingly endless procession of impossible loads being carried pushed, pulled or even rolled back and forth through the streets of the commercial centres and across the Howrah Bridge to the City's principal railway station.

The keenest of the street traders will soon be preparing to set up their stalls along the eastern pavements at the lower end of Rabindra Sarani Some have already arrived with their stock in trade contained in amorphous bundles, waiting for enough light to set out their wares in the most inviting of displays. In an hour or two there will be so much trading along this stretch that there will be no room to walk on the pavement; then those on foot will have to take their chances along the half metre or so of roadway between the kerb and the tram tracks.

The traveller will meet with unfamiliar sights for a City. There will be men herding goats, either one or two or a sizeable herd, along urban thoroughfares, to market or in search of grazing for the day. There may be the occasional cow nosing amongst the vegetable waste in the gutters of side streets. Chickens will be seen running free around the pavement shanties near to where Chitteranjan Avenue meets B.B. Ganguly Street: perhaps not quite free, as careful observation will show a lengthy tether of twine, one end secured to the chicken's leg and the other to convenient pavement railings.

Even at this hour the air will be faintly sticky with heat but, for an hour or two at least, relatively free from that metallic taste and vague haze caused by pollution from motor traffic. That will come later. It is a good time to take in the aromas of Calcutta. The ever present smell of food being prepared, a combination of hot ghee, smoke from open cooking fires mingled with heady mixtures of spices. There is also that slightly sweet and vaguely pleasing background odour of over-ripe fruit and decaying vegetable matter, most noticeable in the lanes and byways near to the food bazaars but carried on any slight breeze to further afield. So too with the smell of incense from the numerous open fronted Hindu shrines where the early risers are performing their first devotions of the day.

There are the distinct sounds of the dawn streets which, in such a brief time will be quite lost amid the all pervading cacophony that is Calcutta in full swing. Quite the loudest of these early sounds is from the ever present multitudes of Crows, perched aloft on the jumbles of telephone lines or hopping arrogantly about anything which appears to them remotely edible. Inter-mingled with their racket are the higher pitched calls of the graceful Kites circling above the buildings. The sounds of human activity too are more discernable at this hour. Metal cooking pots being stirred or scoured; the slap of laundry upon stone, often the paving stones; the gushing of street standpipes at which, already, there are people queuing to perform their ablutions. The thin, high call to early prayer carried from the minaret of the Nakhoda Mosque which lies where Zakaria Street joins Rabindra Sarani. Intermingled with all this is the haunting, almost gentle sound of tram bells; suddenly and rudely shattered as one of these iron monsters comes rattling and grinding around the corner just feet in front of you.

In the slowly gathering half light of approaching dawn, what first appeared as indistinct shapes begin to take on understandable form. That pile of old packing cases, bits of brick, tin, remnants of canvas and plastic sheeting in the corner of Ramesh Dutta Street which, as you passed by twenty minutes ago, you imagined to be rubbish abandoned by some thoughtless fly-tipper, is now, as you re-trace your route, evolving into something rather different. Now you can detect a kind of entrance; you can see that, to one side there is a woman squatting to light a cooking fire, a small child sitting next to her. Behind her is what appears to be a makeshift washing line strung with ragged and faded clothing, being attended to by a young girl carrying a baby held to her hip. What you first took to be a heap of abandoned debris is actually a family's home. Upon this realisation, the western newcomer to Calcutta may experience an unaccountable sense of embarrassment, anxious not to appear to be staring. There is no need; respectful curiosity is a virtue in Calcutta and a wave and friendly smile will, invariably, be returned.

Whilst the sun is still just below the horizon, the traveller should strike out for the great iron Howrah Bridge. There are few better places to be found within the City from which to watch the sun rise. Standing mid-span affords perhaps the most open aspect achievable in central Calcutta, arguably, better even than from the middle of the Maidan. With the sluggish, brown Hooghly flowing beneath, the view northwards beyond the Ahriatola Ghat or southwards beyond Vidyasagar Setu, the second Hooghly bridge, will be shrouded in early mist. This will soon disappear with the rapidly rising sun, whose heat is now becoming distinctly noticeable.

There is no clearer announcement to the start of a new Calcutta day than the steadily growing numbers of people, on foot, on bicycles and crammed into ramshackle buses, streaming across this great iron bridge from Howrah on the western bank, meeting almost equal numbers going in the opposite direction, making for the main railway station and points beyond. Within the hour this will develop into an unstoppable and unceasing tide of humanity which will not begin to abate until long after dark. Then your present leisurely observations from this stationery vantage point will become quite impossible.

CALCUTTA ON FOOT

CHAPTER 1

Around Dalhousie Square
to Old China Bazar Street

This walk takes in the most south westerly of the areas of the
City covered in this work and includes the extent of what was
the European quarter, or 'White Town' as far back as the first
quarter of the 18th century. It contains some of the oldest thoroughfares in Calcutta and is steeped in historical connections.
The nearest metro stations serving this area are Esplanade,
located just south of the Bentinck Street/Lenin Sarani crossing
and Chandni Chowk located close to the Ganesh Chandra
Avenue/Chitteranjan Avenue crossing.

A good starting point is the junction where B. B. Ganguly Street
becomes Lalbazar Street and grand Bentinck Street merges
northwards into the less grand Rabindra Sarani. In the early
18th century this point was known as 'The Cross Roads' and
marked the easternmost boundary of the European quarter. It
is said also that this location was once a place of execution.

Most of northern side of Lalbazar Street is taken up by the
grand edifice housing the headquarters of the Calcutta Police.
This rambling building still includes the central lockup, located
on the side fronting Rabindra Sarani. Behind the Police
Headquarters lies Radha Bazar entered by the Lane of that
name from Rabindra Sarani or via Radha Bazar Street which
branches north off Lalbazar Street, just west of the Police

Headquarters building. This bazaar is the place to go if you are in the market for watches or clocks.

Almost directly opposite the Police Headquarters, on the southern side of Lalbazar Street, there once stood an ancient jail. This was badly damaged in the assault on Calcutta of 1756 [1] and was subsequently demolished.

Heading west along Lalbazar Street, the last turning on the left is R.N. Mukherjee Road. This is one of the oldest roads in Calcutta and was formerly known as Mission Row (and still is by many). Here you will find the old Mission Church, built in 1770 and said to be the first Protestant church in East India.

At an even earlier date this thoroughfare, then known as Rope Walk, contained several magnificent mansions. One of these mansions was the home of the redoubtable Lady Russell who set up and ran the temporary hospital when, in 1756, Fort William was under attack from the massed armies of the Nawab of Bengal.

At the southern end of this thoroughfare, turn right into Ganesh Chandra Avenue then left into Hemanta Bose Sarani (formerly Old Court House Street). On the eastern side of this street stands the once famous Great Eastern Hotel This historic hotel is the oldest in Calcutta and one of the oldest to be found anywhere in India.

The story of this hotel began in 1840 when an Englishman, one David Wilson, established the Auckland Hotel on this site. 'Dainty Davy', as he was apparently known, (although precisely why he attracted this sobriquet is uncertain), named his hotel after the Governor General of the time, Lord Auckland. Despite

---

[1]See Annexe 1 - Historical Notes

this, the hotel became more popularly and widely known as 'Wilson's Hotel'.

In 1865 the hotel was floated as 'The Great Eastern Hotel Wine and General Purveying Company' and grew to become the favoured haunt of Calcutta's social elite. The hotel became a byword for taste, elegance and luxury. So high was this reputation that it was often referred to as the 'Jewel of the East' By the mid 1880's the entire premises had, remarkably, gone over to electric lighting; possibly the first such establishment in the entire sub-continent to do so.

The Great Eastern began a slow decline from the 1960's onwards. By the 1970's this ageing, faded beauty was facing financial ruin, largely as a result of ongoing disputes between the partners. The hotel had to be rescued by first being taken over by the State Government before being finally nationalised in 1980.

As luck would have it, my wife and I were fortunate enough to last stay in the Great Eastern in 2005, the final year of the hotel's operation. The premises were finally sold off at the end of that year to an international hotel chain and have remained closed ever since pending completion of extensive works of modernisation and refurbishment. Mercifully, the fine exterior is to be preserved.

Opposite the frontage of the old Great Eastern is Larkin Lane which, as you walk westwards quickly becomes Pannalal Banerji Lane (once known, intriguingly, as Fancy Lane), before emerging onto Council House Street. Directly opposite is St John's Church or 'The Stone Church' as it is popularly known. The entrance to the grounds of the Church is to be found off the western side of Council House Street close to the junction with K.S. Roy Street. A friendly guard at the gate will relieve you of 10 rupees and issue a ticket which states that your entrance fee helps to relieve the poor of the City and maintain the Church and grounds.

St John's Church was built in the 1780's and so ranks amongst the oldest in Calcutta. It was supposedly built to a plan adapted from London's St Martin-in-the-Fields Church but with modifications designed to minimize load on the soft ground supporting the foundations. The Church and grounds provide a surprisingly tranquil setting given the general hubbub of the surrounding streets.

On one side of the Church is an ornate monument to Lady Charlotte Canning, wife of the East India Company's last Governor General and the Crown's first Viceroy of India. Her actual grave is at Barrackpore an old cantonment settlement some dozen miles upriver from this spot. Within the Church and to the left of the alter, is the magnificent painting by Zofanni, 'The Last Supper'. It is said by some that this is actually a copy rather than the original.

In the Church grounds, just north of the Church itself is a whitewashed, octagonal and domed structure set in a neatly kept area of garden. This is Job Charnock's Mausoleum which was restored from its previously deplorable condition, by the Calcutta Municipal Corporation in 2007. Charnock, who died in 1692, came from Lancashire. He first arrived in India in 1656 although it is not known exactly when he joined the East India Company. He is known to have been trading in Cossimbazar and in Patna before becoming the Company's chief agent at Hooghly in 1685. He moved his operation down river to Sutanuti situated on the east bank of the Hooghly River but, subsequently, had to flee upriver on at least two occasions. He finally settled there permanently in August 1690. It is believed he was led to Sutanuti and the adjoining settlements of Kalikata and Gobindapur by the two powerful families of merchants in yarn and cloth, the Sheths and the Basaks, who had already established themselves at Sutanuti. The location also had distinct defensive advantages with the river one side and salt marshes a few miles east, protecting the landward side.

Whilst Job Charnock is popularly and widely celebrated as the founder of Calcutta this claim is not without controversy. This culminated, in May 2003, in the Calcutta High Court determining, on the basis of an Expert Committee Report, that 'a highly civilised society' and an 'important trading centre' had existed on the site of what became Calcutta, long before the first Europeans arrived. The Court held that, on that basis Job Charnock could not be regarded as the founder of Calcutta. This official line seems to be widely ignored; some would say deservedly so.

Job Charnock's Mausoleum is popularly believed to be the oldest piece of masonry in Calcutta. Around the Mausoleum, set flat in the ground are a number of old tombstones of 18th century origin.

There are other notables interred in Charnock's Mausoleum. William Hamilton, a Surgeon of the East India Company (died December 1717) and who achieved fame for 'curing Ferrukseer the present King of Indostan of a malignant distemper.' For this he was rewarded with 'an elephant, a horse, five thousand rupees in money, two diamond rings, a jewelled aigrette (head-dress decoration), a set of gold buttons and models of all his instruments in gold.' More important, was the influence achieved by the East India Company with the grateful King who went on to grant important rights allowing the Company to establish itself and expand in Bengal.

Twenty metres west of Charnock's Mausoleum, is a similar but smaller domed structure. This is also the last resting place of the remarkable and much married Mrs Frances Johnson; 'the oldest resident of Bengal, universally beloved, respected and revered.' She was born in April 1725 and married her first husband, a Mr Parry Templer at the tender age of 13. He died prematurely. Her second husband, Mr James Althan was even more unlucky, succumbing to smallpox within days of the marriage. Husband number three was a Mr William Watts who lived long enough to produce 4 children with Frances. On his death, Frances remarried in 1774. Her fourth husband, the Rev. 'Tally-Ho' Johnson, at some later point, returned to England whilst Frances chose to stay on in Calcutta. It is said that her whist parties were one of the most sought after social engagements of Calcutta. This extraordinary lady lived on until February 1812 when she died at, for those times, the great age of 87 years.

To the left of the Mausoleum, close up against the boundary wall fronting Church Lane, is another, but less well kept, monument, in the form of an obelisk. This is to the memory of the 123 victims and 23 survivors of 'the Black Hole of Calcutta' [2] who, on the night of 21st June 1756 following the fall of Calcutta, were incarcerated in the 'Black Hole' prison cell of the old Fort William. There is some controversy as to the actual number of those incarcerated; some schools of thought insist a far lower number of between 40 and 70 souls whilst a few diehards deny that the event ever happened at all.

This is not the original monument. The first monument was erected by John Zephaniah Holwell (a survivor and subsequent Governor of Bengal), in 1760. It stood opposite the east gate of the old Fort William close to the spot where the victims of the 'Black Hole' were buried. This was of brick construction and rapidly deteriorated. It was finally pulled down in 1821 and, on the orders of Lord Curzon, replaced in 1901 by the present, marble obelisk. The monument originally stood in Dalhousie Square but was moved to the present location in 1940.

---

[2]See Annexe 1 - Historical Notes

Leaving the Church grounds turn left, back into Council House Street, then walk north until you come to the southern side of Dalhousie Square. The Square was once known as 'Tank Square' and before that 'The Park.' It was later renamed after Lord Dalhousie the Governor General of India from 1848 to 1856. It is now called B.B.D. Bagh; renamed in honour of three young nationalist martyrs, Benoy, Badal and Dinesh who, in September 1930, shot dead the Inspector General of Prisons, N.S. Simpson, at the Writers Building on the northern side of this Square.

The southern side of the Square is dominated by the Telephone Bhavan (the central telephone and telegraph office). On the south west corner stands Hong Kong House, a fine building housing the HSBC bank.

Walking anti-clockwise around the Square, there is a large bus terminus on the eastern side. Another terminus and depot, that of the wonderful Calcutta Tramways Corporation, is sited on the northern side of the Square.

In the centre of the Square stands Lal Dighi, or as the British called it 'the great tank' It is not actually a Dighi (lake) but rather a large pond fed by natural springs. It once provided fish for the table of the Governor's house set within the walls of the old Fort William, once located just to the west. Lal Dighi has been the central feature of the town plan of Calcutta since the City's inception. Today it provides a picturesque and relatively tranquil setting.

Facing the northern side of the Square stands the Writers' Building, so called as the purpose of the original building was to house the clerks (writers) of the East India Company. The existing Writers' Building now houses the offices of the Bengal State Secretariat. It was designed by a Col. St. Clair Wilkins and was completed in 1880. It replaced an earlier, white plastered, structure dating from the 1780's. Before this the 'writers were accommodated within the old Fort William.

Just east of the Writers' Building is the landmark St. Andrew's Church, often referred to as the 'Scottish Church.' The Church stands on the site part occupied in the 18th century by the old Court House. In external design it has many similarities with St. John's Church. The entrance opens on to a flight of stairs flanked by tall pillars and elegant porticos. The Church is fully air conditioned, making it unique amongst churches throughout the City.

Leaving the Church, turn right, walking past the Writers' Building to the north western corner of the Square where it meets Netaji Subhas Road. Just south of this point, on the western side of this road, is the magnificent Calcutta General Post Office. This is an extremely fine, domed building standing over 200 feet high and fronted with Corinthian pillars. It was constructed in the 1860's to a design by Sir Walter Granville.

The site of the General Post Office is of considerable archaeological interest. On the eastern staircase of the building is an inscription which reads 'the lines in the adjacent steps and pavement mark the position and extent of part of the southeast bastion of old Fort William; the extreme south-east point being 95 feet from this wall,' Near the north east corner of the building there used to be a black marble plaque identifying the exact location of the 'Black Hole' prison cell of the old Fort. This plaque was removed many years ago during structural alterations and has not been replaced. In the yard of the Post Office, there were once fragments of the original arcades that lined the east wall of the old Fort but these have since vanished, probably demolished in the course of alterations.

Dotted around in the vicinity of the Post Office will be seen numbers of men armed with primitive typewriters, pens, paper,

envelopes and other impedimenta of their trade, sitting at fold
up tables or upturned crates. These are the letter writers who,
for a nominal fee will formulate letters from the information
provided by their illiterate customers. They will also complete
for their customers any number of the plethora of official forms
which are the lifeblood of Indian bureaucracy and without
which it is all but impossible to access even the most basic services. A little to the south of here, along Esplanade Row West
and K.S. Roy Street, their specialist brothers in trade cater for
those having business with the High Court, the Town Hall or
the State Secretariat all housed close by.

Bapan Soutra has been in the business for nearly twenty years,
acting not only as scribe but also as a kind of confidant and advi-
sor to his unlettered customers. He says his clients were found
mainly from among the hosts of illiterate migrant workers
drawn to Calcutta from the impoverished hinterlands of Bengal
and beyond in search of work. The letters he transcribed for his
customers and the remittances enclosed, often provided the
only source of communication and means of support between
them and the families they left behind with only rare return
visits possible. Mr Soutra was pessimistic about the future,
citing the enormous surge in availability of mobile phones and
the growth of sophisticated electronic cash remittance services,
as amongst the reasons for a fall off in his trade in recent years.

Continuing northwards up Netaji Subhas Road you first pass
the side of the Writers' Building to your right then the Reserve
Bank of India and the junction with Fairlie Place on your left.
The next turning on the right is the western end of India
Exchange Place. About half way down and to the left, is the
beginning of Old China Bazar Street. This ancient and madly
congested thoroughfare is a delight to explore.

Walking north up Old China Bazar Street, first cross the junction of B.R.B. Bose Road, (the old Canning Street). The second

turning on the right after this junction is Synagogue Street, a reminder of Calcutta's long established but now dwindling Jewish population, Further reminders are to be found in the Synagogues located in nearby B.R.B Bose Road and Pollack Street, running north of Radha Bazar Street.

Take the next turning on the right past Synagogue Street into the short, western arm of Armenian Street. Here the Armenian Church rises splendidly above the surrounding, tightly packed buildings. The northern entrance to the Church is to be found, though with some difficulty for it is discreet, directly opposite number 45 (Champalal & Sons) and immediately to the right of number 2 (F.K. Trading). There is also a western entrance off Old China Bazar Street. This is even more difficult to locate buried as it is amongst the clusters of small traders and throngs of people,

A plaque at the northern entrance puts the date of construction of the Church at 1724, although it is not clear whether this relates to the original, wooden structure which stood on this site. Nevertheless, the Church must rank as one of the oldest, if not the oldest, in Calcutta. The Church was built on land purchased by a wealthy merchant to provide a cemetery for the Armenian community of Calcutta. The immaculately kept churchyard is paved with gravestones, many with inscriptions in both the Armenian script and in English. There is one particular grave which is still the subject of much controversy. It stands in front of the main building and is inscribed 'This is the tomb of Reza Bibi, wife of the late charitable Sookias who departed from this world to life eternal.' Another inscription is in the Armenian script. One researcher, Mesior Je Seth, who authored a book on the Armenians of Calcutta, deciphered the grave's Armenian inscription as dating to 1630. If this is accurate, (and there those who dispute it), this would have put the Armenians in Calcutta long before Job Charnock anchored his ships and planted the British flag on the east bank of the Hooghly at Sutanuti.

The Church seems smaller internally than the outside proportions suggest but together with the grounds, form an oasis of tranquillity amidst the pulsating melee which surrounds it.

For those wishing to return to their starting point, the shortest route is east along Armenian Street, turning right into Brabourne Road, then continue walking south past the junction with B.R.B. Bose Road, until you return to St Andrew's Church on your right and Lalbazar Street on your left. A short distance east along Lalbazar Street brings you back to the Rabindra Sarani/Bentinck Street crossing.

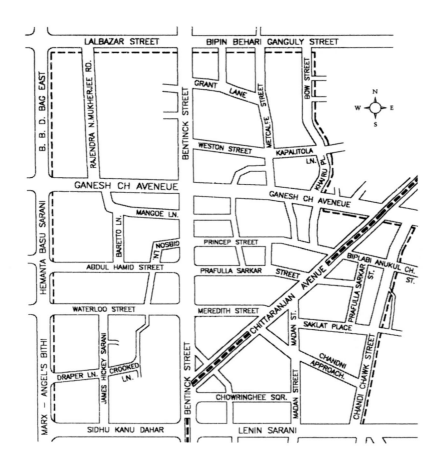

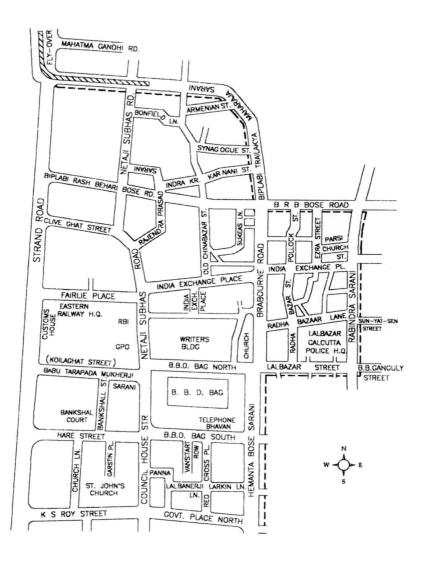

Chapter 2

Jorasanko (South) and Bow Bazar

This walk takes in two very distinct but adjacent areas. The first, the area centred around College Street, lies to the east of Chitteranjan Avenue, the other, part of Bow Bazar and the south eastern fringe of Burra Bazar, lies to the west.

College Street and environs, with its relatively wide thoroughfares is regarded as the intellectual heart of Calcutta, a centre of learning and culture and the location of some of the most respected academic institutions in India. Bow Bazar (or rather this section of it as the remainder will be dealt with in another walk described in Chapter 6), is, by contrast, a maze of ancient lanes taking in Tiretta Bazar and what is left of Calcutta's old, central Chinatown.

A convenient starting point for this walk is the very busy junction where Mahatma Gandhi Road (M.G. Road) crosses Chitteranjan Avenue, (popularly called C.R Avenue, or 'Central'). This junction lays just a few hundred metres south of the M.G. Road metro station.

An early part of the suggested route takes in College Street, famous for its bookshops, publishing houses and most of all, second-hand book stalls. It is known locally as 'Boi Para', or book neighbourhood. Unlike most of the rest of Calcutta, College Street, most likely because of the proximity of numerous academic institutions, is not an early riser. The Street never seems to get fully into swing before about 10.30 a.m. when the second-hand book stalls begin to open. It is as well to time the walk accordingly or even reverse the route so as to allow for this.

From the starting point, head east along M.G. Road. After a hundred metres or so, look to the left hand side of the Road where you will find number 99, easily identifiable by the shop front nameplate on the ground floor, 'The Bengal Dyeing, Cleaning and Shawl Repairing Works.' This building has an elaborate and interesting facade with intricate ironwork balconies. It rises through five storeys in red brick with faked stone dressings. There is a different arch design to the windows at each level, some incorporating fanlights. The facade sports mock Doric columns with Grecian urns thrown in for good measure. Architecturally eccentric is perhaps the best overall description but nevertheless very pleasing and a good example of the more grandiose 19th century buildings of central and north Calcutta. Unfortunately, it appears to be in a very bad state of repair.

Continuing eastwards, the next main junction is College Street. To the left there once stood the old College Street market, now cleared for development as the country's first integrated book mall. Several hundred traders were displaced by this closure, although many of the larger concerns are being accommodated in nearby Marcus Square. Some, but by no means all, will return to the redeveloped College Street on completion of the redevelopment project.

Turning right and walking south down College Street, both sides of the thoroughfare and some of the side streets are lined with hundreds of bookstalls, their stock spilling over onto the pavements. Some of the stalls are tiny, not much more than a cubby hole or tray sized table, others much larger and dealing in both new and second-hand books. There are books on, seemingly, every conceivable subject to be found here and it is perhaps the only place in the entire City, where the traders seem content to let potential customers browse unmolested and at leisure, without strident imprecations to purchase.

College Street is widely regarded as the nerve centre of Calcutta's intelligentsia. There is a coffee shop here which is a favourite haunt of young Bengali intellectuals and where, I am told, you can enjoy the best political arguments to be had anywhere in the City.

There are some fine buildings along College Street housing the academic and medical institutions which abound in this quarter. The first such building on the right is the Presidency College, one of the affiliated and co-founding colleges of Calcutta University. It is one of oldest colleges in India and is consistently rated in the highest achieving ten percent of such establishments in the entire sub-continent. Established in 1817 as the Hindu College, it was originally housed in the Chitpore Road (present day Rabindra Sarani). In 1830 the College moved to Bow Bazar and later to the building which now houses the Sanskit College, located further south on the op-posite side of College Street. The Hindu College was renamed Presidency College in 1855, from which date it was open to students from all communities.

Next to the College, on the same side of the road, is the Hare School. This famous establishment is one of the oldest extant schools in India. It was founded in 1818 by a Scottish watch-maker, David Hare, with the help of the great social reformer of the day, Raja Ram Mohan Roy. These two men were to feature prominently in the development of educational provi-sion in the City. The School was originally known as Arpuli Pathshala, later becoming the Kalutola Branch School. It became known by its present name from around 1865.

Almost directly opposite the Hare School is the highly reputed, Hindu School, established in 1817. The original, very much smaller building still stands within the grounds, as does the Sanskrit College which was founded in 1835.

Just south of the Hindu School is College Square, a pleasant and relatively peaceful open space which includes a large swimming pool.

Opposite College Square is the Centenary and Asutosh Buildings of the College Street campus of Calcutta University. There are several other campuses scattered throughout the City. The University was established in 1857 and was the first modern university in the sub-continent. Indeed it was the first university, east of Suez, to teach European classics, English literature and occidental and oriental philosophy and history. India's first Nobel Laureate, the great writer and poet, Rabindranath Tagore is one of the University's noted alumni. The University has a long and proud history of providing coeducational opportunity. The first women's college, Bethune College was opened in 1879 and in 1882, two young ladies, Chandramuki Basu and Kadambini Ganguly, became the first women university graduates in India.

Next door to the campus lies the Ezra Hospital, founded in 1888, originally for the treatment of the City's Jewish population. It is now incorporated into the Calcutta Medical College and Hospital, whose sprawling complex begins next door. The Medical College was founded in 1835 and was the first such establishment in the whole of Asia to teach European medical science.

Continue south along College Street, taking the first turning on the right into Eden Hospital Road. On the right are further wings of the Medical College and Hospital complex, including the main Nurses Hostel. To the left are the offices of the Azad

Hind, the Urdu, daily newspaper. Close by, Eden Hospital Road joins Chitteranjan Avenue. Looking north along Chitteranjan Avenue, Eden Hospital can be seen to your right. This women's hospital was established in 1881 and is now also part of the Medical College and Hospital.

Turn left into Chitteranjan Avenue and walk south until you come to the junction with B.B. Ganguly Street (formerly Bow Bazar Street) which runs both east and west of this point. On each of the four corners of this junction are entrances to Central metro station. There is also a manned, controlled crossing here by which you can cross Chitteranjan Avenue, in relative safety, to the western arm of B.B. Ganguly Street. Standing here, outside the Bow Bazar post office, you are now at the south eastern corner of what is left of Calcutta's central Chinatown. This lies within the maze of ancient lanes stretching northwards from here to Colotolla Street.

Chinese migration to Calcutta began in the late 18th century. The early migrants were mainly Cantonese and settled in this area. Later migrants, traditionally shoe makers and leather tanners, settled in Calcutta's second Chinatown at Tangra. This is located in the eastern suburbs of the City just north of Gobra and is where the majority of Calcutta's remaining Chinese community now reside.

The decline of central Chinatown really dates from the early 1960's. This was a time of great tension between India and China over border issues which led to their first armed conflict in 1962.[3] As a result of these hostilities, many of the Chinese community were interned in camps in far away Rajasthan. Those remaining in Calcutta now regarded their future prospects in the City as bleak and many chose to leave India for Australia, Canada, USA and the UK. Many of those interned

---

[3]See Annexe 1 - Historical Notes

followed suit upon release. Coupled with this was the physical decimation of Chinatown by the Calcutta Improvement Trust's wholesale demolitions in the area to facilitate the laying out of new thoroughfares, India Exchange Place Extension and New C.I.T. Road and a number of high rise office blocks. However, not everyone left. Today, there still remains some vestige of the old Chinatown and a tenacious but very much reduced Chinese community.

From outside Bow Bazar post office, continue west along B.B. Ganguly Street until, on the right, you come to The Beeu Hotel, a modern, building and rather incongruous in this setting but having a very good restaurant. This structure now occupies the site of the Bow Bazar bomb blast which, in March 1993, killed 69 people and injured many others. The original building on this site, owned by Mohamed Rashid Khan, a shady under-world personality, was being used to store explosives and ammunition, presumably the tools of his trade. He and five co-conspirators were convicted and received life sentences.

This thoroughfare, in ancient times was known as the 'Avenue' or 'Avenue to the eastward.' It later became known as Bow Bazar Street, before being renamed Bipin Behari (B.B. for short), Ganguly Street, in honour of the revolutionary leader of that name who spent more than 20 years in British Indian jails and later joined the Congress movement.

Continuing westward, you come to Hide Lane on the right. This leads into Phears Lane and two of the remaining three, fragmented arms of Blackburn Lane, the very heart of what was old Chinatown. Instead of this route, walk past the entrance to Hide Lane and take the next turning on your right. This is Chatawala Gullee, sometimes spelt Chhattawala Gali. Such has been the past reputation of this narrow, congested lane that I have heard it said that, in bygone days, teachers and parents exasperated at some errant behaviour of their young charges, would frequently threaten banishment to this place: in the imagination, the lowest pit of hell to which everything wicked was relegated. The Gullee has two arms. From where you have entered it runs north until it reaches Sun-Yat-Sen Street. About half way along this stretch, the Gullee also branches to the left and right. The left hand branch exits onto Rabindra Sarani whilst the right hand branch, narrowing to little more than a pathway, leads out a little further east along Sun-Yet-Sen Street.

It is well worth spending a little time taking in everything that goes on here and there is much to see. It takes a leap of the imagination to see how the visible numbers of people cooking, washing, chatting, playing or just idling outdoors all along the Gullee can possibly be accommodated within the buildings here. This becomes more of a mystery when you realise that the ground floors of most of these buildings are given over to small industry. There are 'factories' for the washing and recycling of plastic bottles; wire stripping and other scavenged metals and paper bag manufacturing; there is even an enterprise turning out large quantities of rice noodles. Reputedly, the Gullee also housed at least one opium den in the old days. Your presence here will arouse considerable, good natured curiosity particularly amongst the numerous children. Be prepared to take more photographs than you intended.

Leaving Chatawala Gullee by either the northern or western arm will bring you out into Sun-Yat-Sen Street. Opposite, on the northern pavement is the Hap Heng Grocery Store, an old, long established Chinese outlet. The street apparently, now bears little resemblance to how it appeared up to the 1950's. I discover from my conversation with Wang Liang Toon, an elderly Chinese gentleman gifted with long memory, that it was then much narrower, hemmed in on all sides by hundreds of small tiled hutments. Mr Toon was born in the area and has lived here all his life as did his father before him.

His grandfather first settled in Calcutta in the 1880's after migrating from China's Canton province. Mr Toon's three sons all live abroad, two in Canada and one in Australia. 'They have mostly all gone from here now, the younger people' he said wistfully.

Walking east along Sun-Yat-Sen Street, there are three short thoroughfares to your left, all called C.I.T. Road. These, together with two of the remaining three fragments of Blackburn Lane, which run both to the left and the right off this street, are the site of some of the most dreadful pavement settlements to be found anywhere in the City. All of these five short thoroughfares lead northwards into India Exchange Place Extension, which becomes New C.I.T. Road towards the eastern end. This was laid out in the early 1960's, involving the wholesale demolitions which fragmented and virtually destroyed the old Chinatown. There are some reminders, for along this road you will find Pouchong Bros. Chinese Sauce Manufacturers and the Sing Cheung Sauce Factory which occupies the same premises as it did when first established way back in 1954.

Here you can also find some interesting pavement industries. One in particular, a family, wood-chopping enterprise, is worthy of note. Here a whole extended family is busily engaged in chopping up old packing cases, pallets and any other timber they can salvage: all, from grandmother to quite young children, wielding menacing looking hatchets, reducing the timber to kindling sized pieces which is sold locally as fuel for cooking fires. The delivery arm of this enterprise is Sati Devi, an engaging, slimly built, young Bihari lady. She stands no taller than 1.5 metres in her chappals and it is likely, weighs less than the huge baskets of kindling she hoists onto her head for delivery to customers in the locality. I lifted one of these filled baskets which could not have weighed less than 40 kilos. The family assured me she was very strong: I did not doubt it.

India Exchange Place extension is dominated by two multi-storey office buildings, hugely overbearing in proportion to surrounding buildings. One of these is the C.I.T Building, the other, the BSNL Telephone Exchange. Squashed between and to the rear of these buildings, survives the premises of the See Ip Association and Temple. The Temple is to be found on the first floor with the ground floor in use as a community centre catering for the, mainly, elderly members of the remaining Chinese community. Visitors to the Temple are welcomed; simply walk on up.

The remaining final, and longest, fragment of Blackburn Lane runs immediately behind the C.I.T Building and the Telephone Exchange. Here, at number 22, close by the See Ip Temple, is where the famous 'Nanking Restaurant' once operated from the ground floor; the upper floor being the Toong On Church. The once grand 'Nanking' from its heyday in the second quarter the 20th century, had, by the 1970's deteriorated to the point that it was widely considered a disreputable place to be seen. The restaurant closed around this time and none has operated from these premises since. The Church on the first floor continued to operate for some years until that too closed. The entire premises now stand empty and there is a very real risk that this fine old building could be lost to development.

At the western end of Blackburn Lane, the narrow Harinbari 3rd Lane leads north towards Tiretta Bazar Lane which, westwards, joins the 'main' Harinbari Lane. This is a red light district, safe enough to walk during the day but inadvisable after dark.

Another route is via Damzen Lane which is to be found about half way along Blackburn Lane, on the northern side. This whole maze of lanes leading north off Blackburn Lane seem almost frozen in time. Other than the modern advertising signs, little else seems to have changed since the 19th century. Notice particularly, the many old houses with open verandas at first floor level. Damzen Lane takes a sharp right turn before it crosses Kalutola Lane and a little further on meets Srinath Babu Lane. Turn left here and after about 100 metres you come to a busy junction. This is where Phears Lane, an ancient, frantically busy, commercial thoroughfare which bisects the whole of this area, runs north to Colotolla Street and south towards B.B. Ganguly Street.

The first turning on your left at this junction is Tiretta Bazar Lane. Walking westward you cross Harinbari Lane and, straight ahead join the short stretch of Tiretta Bazar Street leading out onto Rabindra Sarani. The Tiretta Bazar is to your right and occupies the entire block between here and Colotolla Street to the north. This sprawling, general bazaar really merits a separate visit to do it justice as you can easily spend a few hours exploring the labyrinth of narrow walkways between the numerous traders and small workshops.

On a pavement outside a cell phone shop in Tiretta Bazar, lives Jamila Khatun, a diminutive woman in her late 30's and handicapped by a lame left leg, a legacy from childhood polio. Orphaned at the age of 9, and widowed when her two children were still babies, this remarkable and resourceful woman, gleaning a meagre living as a sweeper, managed to send both her children to school for an education she never had any chance of receiving herself. A recipient of an award for excellence in The Telegraph Newspaper's School Awards, this lady's tenacity and sheer determination is nothing short of astonishing.

Tiretta Bazar occupies the south eastern corner of the busy junction where Colotolla Street joins Rabindra Sarani from the east and Biplabi Rash Behari Basu Road from the west. This junction also marks the approximate boundary where Bow Bazar ends and Burra Bazar begins. As you walk north up Rabindra Sarani it becomes increasingly difficult to keep to the pavement which is so jam-packed with traders and their wares that there is hardly room to move. Dominating the right hand side of the road, and standing at the junction with Zakaria Street, is the towering, green domed Nakhoda Mosque. This magnificent red sandstone edifice was built in the 1920's and is modelled on the mausoleum of the Mughal Emperor Akbar at Secundra. The domes and minarets rise to 150 feet above street level. Internally the mosque is a monument to the Islamic decorative arts. The enormous prayer hall can accommodate up to ten thousand. The gateway of the Mosque is built in the style of the Buland Darwaza (Persian for high or great gate) which Akbar had built at Fetephur Sikri, near Agra.

Turning into Zakaria Street, walk eastwards to the second turning on your left, N. Badruddin Street. This will take you north, past Tara Chand Dutta Street on your right, to Mahatma Ghandi Road (M.G. Road) For those that have the time, the whole length of Zakaria Street and Tara Chand Dutta Street are worth exploring as both are thriving hubs of small scale manufacturing and frenetic trading. This short detour, involves continuing eastwards along Zakaria Street and taking the last turning on the left into Syed Sally Lane. About 100 metres north, this lane joins with Tara Chand Dutta Street where, if you turn left you rejoin N. Badruddin Street and your original route out onto M.G. Road.

Just before you exit onto M.G. Road, particularly if before noon, you will pass by one of the biggest middens in the City. Here, workers of the Calcutta Municipal Corporation, aided by a JCB excavator or two, will be shovelling the mountains of refuse into waiting trucks, to be taken to the dumping grounds of Dhapa out in the City's eastern suburbs. Most of this waste comes from the huge Mechua fruit market which lies just behind the northern frontage of M.G. Road. This huge midden is cleared and replenished on a daily basis.

Turning right into M.G. Road, you soon come to a heavily fortified 'Off Shop'. Here you can purchase a wide variety of wines, beers and spirits provided you are prepared to conduct your business through a heavy iron grill which would do justice to a bullion vault.

A little further along is the Himalay Hotel and the attached, vegetarian restaurant, 'Girnaar'. The food here is excellent, particularly the fine lunchtime thalis.

Just past the 'Girnaar' is the pavement pitch of the charming and avuncular Mr Bishu Das. Mr Das is by calling, an astrologer and palmist. Armed with the tools of his trade all packed in a small neat wooden chest, he squats there receiving his clients from early morning until sunset, revealing to them their 'past, present and future,' as he puts it. Between clients, he will be seen studiously consulting his texts and charts.

A little further on and you come to the M.G. Road, Chitteranjan Avenue crossing, the starting point for this walk. From here, M.G. Road metro station is a few hundred metres north along Chitteranjan Avenue and Central metro station a little further than this southwards.

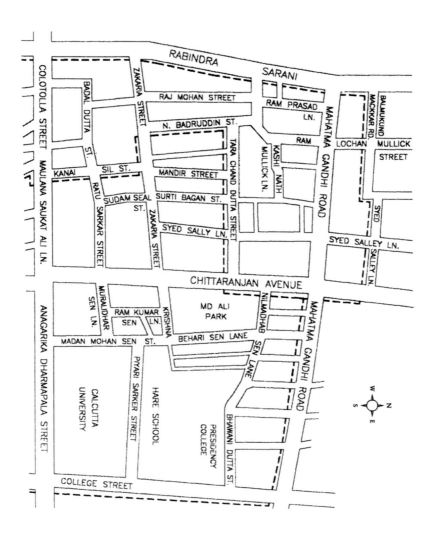

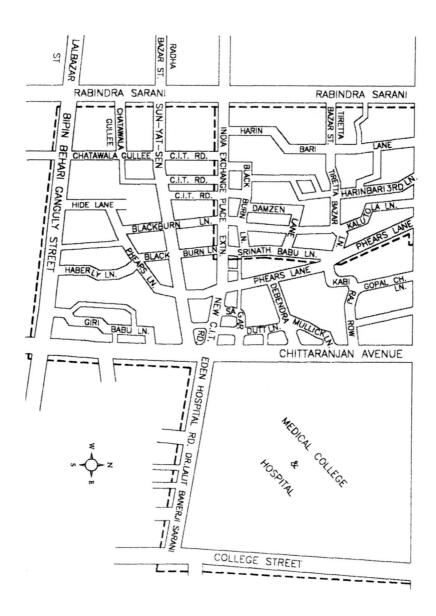

CHAPTER 3

Around Burra Bazar
and the Howrah Bridge

This walk includes the Howrah Bridge and takes in almost the entirety of Burra Bazar, (sometimes spelt Bara Bazar), the commercial heart of Calcutta and one of the largest wholesale and retail market complexes in India. The small area omitted here is the Old China Bazar Street and Armenian Church locale which was covered in the walk described at Chapter 1.

Burra Bazar covers the area which lies between Canning Street in the south, Kali Krishna Tagore Street in the north, Rabindra Sarani to the east and the River Hooghly to the west. The entire area is dissected by Mahatma Ghandi Road (M.G. Road) which runs, centrally, east to west. It is often said that within this rough geographical area, Burra Bazar is a world in itself. Where 'anything and everything is available even tiger's milk if you pay the right price.' It was also the streets and lanes of this area which witnessed some of the worst excesses of the dreadful riots which raged through Calcutta in 1946.[4]

The area is served by M.G. Road metro station located in Chitteranjan Avenue, a few hundred metres north of the M.G. Road crossing.

---

[4]See Annexe 1 - Historical Notes

There are records showing a concentration of trading activity in this area from at least the very beginning of the 18th century. In those days this market area was known as Sutanuti haat, later coming to be known as Bazar Kolkata. It must have been a sizeable centre of commerce as records show the market to have extended to about 18 hectares with a residential area spread over a further 14 hectares, located just to the north around Jorabagan. The whole area was sacked and largely destroyed in the assault on Calcutta in 1756 by the armies of the Nawab of Bengal. Records left by those besieged in the old Fort William, tell of fires from the market area, clearly visible from the Fort, which raged throughout the night and early hours of 17/18th June of that year.

From around the middle of the 19th century, Burra Bazar began to grow as the stronghold of the Marwari businessmen, originating from Rajastan. Stage by stage the Marwaris replaced first the Bengalis then the Hindi speaking Khatris. By the 1870's they had gained control over the inland trade in jute and cotton goods and within the next two decades had virtually monopolized the indigenous banking system. Whilst Burra Bazar today remains a Marwari stronghold, from the 1970's the very wealthiest began migrating out of the area to neighbourhoods such as Alipore and Ballygunge and started to relocate their offices to the Dalhousie Square area.

Burra Bazar is divided into a number of sub-markets, (patties) according to the goods principally traded, hence Dhotipatti, Fancypatti, Tulapatti and so on. Further sub-divisions are katra, chowk or kothi, although so congested and frenetic is the whole area that it is all but impossible to determine with any accuracy where one sub-division ends and another begins; a subtle change in the predominant type of goods being traded is about the only clue.

Over the years, many of the once large trading outlets have been sub-divided into numerous very small shops or warehouses.

This coupled with the plethora of illegal and jerry built extensions and other questionable development has turned many of the buildings in Burra Bazar into veritable warrens. You can enter these buildings from one lane, get hopelessly lost in the narrow twisting maze of corridors and stairwells within and emerge into an entirely different lane.

Civic records show that of every one hundred buildings in Burra Bazar, eighty are illegal in the sense that they have been built or extended without any planning or building consents. Buildings have been extended both vertically and horizontally with scant regard to structural integrity or access arrangements in the already crowded narrow lanes that make up much of the area. The Calcutta Municipal Corporation estimates that around 600 buildings in Burra Bazar can be classed as hazardous whilst a further 500 are considered medium to high risk. The West Bengal Fire Service cites the collapse of 5 buildings and partial collapse of 30 others in 2007 alone. In nearly all of these buildings 50 to 100 tiny shops had been built on each floor by erecting plywood partitions.

A convenient starting point for this walk is at the south east corner of the area where Biplabi Rash Behari Bose Road (Canning Street), meets Rabindra Sarani. This point is about equidistant between M.G. Road and Central metro stations and about 100 metres south of the landmark Nakhoda Mosque.

From here walk west along Canning Street to the first turning on the right, which is Amratola Street. At this junction stands the Bagri Market (the actual address of which is 71 Canning Street). The Market, which is both wholesale and retail, does a roaring trade in brightly coloured plastic toys of all descriptions. If you are here around the time of Holi, (the Festival of Colours) you will see mountains of plastic water pistols, essential for dousing friends and family in the colours so integral to the Festival. The market also deals in stationery, glassware, various foodstuffs and, oddly, moulded luggage.

Just past the Bagri Market, turn right into Amratola Street and walk northwards, passing Amratola Lane on the right, until you come to the junction with Armenian Street. This street runs both east and west from here. The route lays westwards but, given time, it is well worth first walking to the eastern end where it joins Rabindra Sarani, then retracing your steps westwards all the way to the other end of the street where it joins Brabourne Road. It will be worth the effort for Armenian Street is an ancient, narrow, commercial thoroughfare which, in full swing, must rank as the most crazily congested in all of Calcutta. Here there are pedestrians, both with and without huge and unwieldy loads, overloaded barrows being pushed or pulled, bicycles, rickshaws, motor cycles, taxis, cars, delivery vans and lorries. Weaving amongst all this are itinerant hawkers, the odd goat and the ever present posse of pariah dogs. I was once here when the whole unruly free-for-all just ground to a complete halt. Locked solid, nothing, not even the unencumbered pedestrian, could move for upwards of ten minutes. Barrows tried to inch by rickshaws, bicycles were scraped along walls, loads were passed overhead to free up space; all to the accompaniment of the vigorous use of vehicle horns. Then, as if some giant plug had been pulled, everything began to move, to the sound of loud cheers and the joyous ringing of bells by the freed cyclists and rickshaw pullers.

Leaving the western end of Armenian Street brings you onto the curve of Brabourne Road. A further short stretch of Armenian Street is to be found starting on the opposite side of Brabourne Road and this was included in the walk described in Chapter 1. Looking south from here affords a view of the magnificent Cathedral Church of our Lady of the Rosary, often called the 'Portuguese Church'. The Church was built in the closing years of the 18th century and replaced an earlier chapel on the site. Portuguese Street runs along the eastern flank of the Church.

A short walk north along Brabourne Road brings you to the junction with Murarka Street, the first turning on right after Armenian Street. Walking north up Murarka Street, the whole block to your left, which contains the Nandaram Market, was ravaged by a huge fire in January, 2008. The fire began in a medicine godown (warehouse) along this street and rapidly engulfed and completely destroyed several areas of the market before spreading to the multi-storey Kashiram block. The fire raged for more than forty hours and destroyed over 1,200 businesses. At the height of the inferno, more than 1,000 people living in neighbouring residential apartments had to be evacuated by the City's emergency services. Many believed this was a catastrophe waiting to happen as the multi-storey market had been illegally extended over the years by the addition of numerous extra storeys. As long ago as 1986, the Supreme Court had declared the whole building illegal as a result of which the Calcutta Municipal Corporation, between 1988 and 1993, demolished the 15th to 21st storeys. The traders struck back and in an effort to prevent any further demolition, the staircase between the 10th and 11th storeys was removed and a bamboo ladder substituted. Whenever the Corporation's inspectors arrived, traders on the lower floors would press a bell and those on the 11th storey would pull up the ladder denying access.

Continue north along Murarka Street, crossing the junction with Jamunalal Bajaj Street, until you come to Mahatma Ghandi Road (M.G. Road). This thoroughfare was once known as Harrison Road, named after Sir Henry Harrison chairman of the Calcutta Municipal Corporation at the time the road was originally conceived and constructed, between 1889 and 1892. This road, which cuts right through Burra Bazar, links Sealdah railway station to the east with the Howrah Bridge approach to the west. The construction of this road swept away whole swathes of festering lanes and teeming slums; much the same as did the contemporaneous laying out of New Oxford Street and High Holborn in London which obliterated the Seven Dials and other similarly insalubrious warrens. Curiously, M.G. Road, south of the Chitteranjan Avenue crossing, is in some ways vaguely reminiscent of High Holborn, both sharing a similar width of carriageway and height and mass of the buildings lining either side.

M.G. Road, being the main artery through Burra Bazar and linking the City's two main railway stations, is one of the best places in Calcutta to stand and simply wonder at the unbelievable amount of goods which are moved around the City by purely manual means. From dawn until well after sunset, there is a seemingly endless procession of incredible loads of every description being carried, pushed or pulled along this thoroughfare. You will see the coolie, in graceful stride to or from the Mechua fruit market, balancing on his head what looks like half the crop of a banana tree or a small haystack of paddy. Another will be going in the opposite direction holding aloft a gross or more of vividly coloured plastic pots all contained in a huge netting bundle. There was one I saw regularly who would be rolling along two large lorry tyres. How he managed this amidst the chaotic traffic of this busy thoroughfare is nothing short of miraculous. So intrigued was I at his amazing skill, that one day I decided to follow him. Even for the first few hundred metres, I had the greatest difficulty in keeping up and finally lost all sight of him amidst the teeming throng as he turned into Rabindra Sarani.

On the left hand side of M.G. Road, just west of the junction with Netaji Subhas Road, stands the Raja Katra, one of the oldest wholesale markets in Calcutta and so named as the site was once owned by the Maharaja of Burdwan. This busy, sprawling market hosts more than six hundred traders dealing in a variety of goods such as cigarettes, paan, betel leaf, betel nut, candles, soap and stationery. This, like nearly all the markets making up Burra Bazar, also has a residential element. Upwards of three thousand people are said to be accommodated with the perimeters of the Raja Katra site.

A little further west M.G. Road ends where it meets Strand Road. Above is the Strand Road flyover which carries road traffic from Brabourne Road to the Howrah Bridge approach. Walking under the flyover you can cross to the western pavement of Strand Road via a manned and controlled crossing. Walking north, Strand Road begins a gradual incline. Around this point you begin to notice that what looks like half the City's populace is streaming towards you, with the other half straining at your heels. This is the approach to one of the busiest bridges on earth, the massive and iconic Howrah Bridge. This was officially renamed Rabindra Setu in 1965, in honour of India's first Nobel Laureate, Rabindranath Tagore.

The Bridge, which links Howrah on the western bank of the Hooghly with Calcutta proper on the eastern bank, was constructed between 1937 and 1943. It replaced a floating pontoon bridge built in 1874 by Sir Bradford Leslie. This earlier bridge had hinged shore spans to accommodate the Hooghly's tides. At the highest tides these spans became so steep that bullock carts (which as late as 1910 made up more than half of vehicular traffic) were unable to negotiate passage. This bridge could also be opened to let river traffic through but was clearly inadequate to cope with the rapidly expanding traffic between Howrah and Calcutta.

Recognition of the need for a new bridge stretched back to the early years of the 20th century but more than three decades of indecision by the Government of Bengal were to pass before the designs of consultant engineers, Rendel, Palmer and Tritton for a replacement suspension type, balanced cantilever bridge were accepted.

Frustration at such delays is perhaps best summed up by an anonymous Englishman, 'Diogenes' in the following poem which appeared in the Calcutta Municipal Gazette in July 1925.

'I stood on the Bridge at midnight,
And gazed at the waters below,
And thought of the fanciful dreams that
From the brains of our Councillors flow.

Then I thought of the quick intuition,
Which these schemes had engendered and said,
Will these schemes ever come to fruition?
Then I quietly stood on my head

For I'd looked at the question sideways,
And from both sides of the town,
Taking careful account of the tideways,
But never from upside down.

So I've got a new angle of vision
As bright and as fresh as wet paint,
Which will take off the general attention
Away from the New Market Saint.

Up my sleeve I've another red herring,
The Scare of the Bidyadhari Silt,
Which will merrily keep the ball rolling
Ere The bridge on the Hooghly is built.

The new bridge was constructed by Cleveland Bridge & Engineering Co. Ltd of Darlington. A total of 26,500 tons of steel were used in the construction, nearly all of which was supplied by the Indian firm of Tata Iron and Steel Co. Fabrication of the steel was undertaken by Braithwaite, Burn & Jessop Co. at several different workshops throughout Calcutta.

The bridge is approximately 700 metres long and 30 metres wide with the two main supporting towers rising to nearly 90 metres. It is said that on a hot day the bridge expands by as much as 100 centimetres (although I have heard of more improbable claims of up to 1 metre).

The level of traffic carried by the bridge is phenomenal, with current census surveys showing a daily total of 150,000 vehicles of all descriptions and a staggering 3 million pedestrian movements. Up until the early 1990's the roadway of the bridge also carried trams across, to and from Howrah Station.

No trip to Calcutta can be complete without a crossing of this great iron bridge, on foot of course. There is a generous footpath provided each side of the bridge, of which almost every square inch will be in use from early morning until well after dark. Cross on one footpath and return on the other. On the outward leg, stick to the southern footpath from where, looking over the parapet to your left, can be seen the Mulick Ghat wholesale flower market spread out in a riot of colours below. Some of the market buildings were badly damaged by fire in April 2008 and whilst there are tentative plans for redevelopment of the site, the future for this market is at present uncertain. Next to the market is the Armenian Ghat where muscled fitness enthusiasts can be seen going through their exercise routines.

Whatever can be carried or carted and much that seems improbable is ferried back and forth across the bridge in a seemingly endless procession between the markets of Burra Bazar and the railway station and warehouses of Howrah. If you are lucky you will even see the occasional coolie expertly rolling along a large hoop made up of coiled piping or cable. You will also find at each end of the bridge skilful exponents of the ancient and ingenious art of 'Kili Josiyam' or, fortune telling with parrots. How this practice came about or who thought it up has probably been lost in the mists of time; if indeed it was ever known at all. There are some who say it originated in the southern state of Tamil Nadu. It works like this. The artiste (for no lesser term does his performance justice), sits with his caged, small green parrot and his pack of fortune telling cards. Those seeking a consultation squat beside him on his pavement pitch, whereupon the parrot is summoned from its cage. The parrot is first told your name and sometimes even your date of birth. The parrot then proceeds to flip over with its beak and one at a time, cards from the pack. When the parrot finds a card considered suitable, it carries it in its beak and hands it over to its master and co-conspirator. The selected card is then interpreted for you; it contains your fate which, in essence, is all down to the given mood of the parrot. There are a number of variations. Some practitioners train their parrots to walk once around their cage each time a card is flipped over; some parrots seem to flip over almost the entire pack before selecting a card, most likely for added dramatic effect. For the usual, trifling consultation fee you can enjoy an experience that restores one's faith in humanity's wonderful inventiveness.

For reasons which will be incomprehensible to the western traveller, you are forbidden to photograph the Howrah Bridge. Much the same prohibition applies to every other government structure or building throughout India whether it be a nuclear installation, rocket base or the staff canteens of weights and measures inspectors. No doubt some dispensation must have been given for the numerous picture postcards of the bridge widely available from most City bookshops.

The best view by far of the bridge is from the river, mid stream. Regular river ferries operate from the ferry ghat on the Howrah side. The ticket office and entrance to the ferry ghat is located just south of the bathing ghat and almost directly opposite the old railway station building.

Recrossing the bridge to the Calcutta side, regain and cross Strand Road to the eastern footpath. Walk a little way northwards and on your right you will see the magnificent frontage of the Old Mint. This was once the main silver and copper mint of India and one of the busiest in the world. Many of the medals and decorations of British India were also produced here. The Old Mint ceased operation in 1952 and the intervening years of disuse and neglect have taken their toll on this now derelict but still stunning building. Built in the Grecian Doric style, the Mint was completed in 1824 and is said to be modelled on the Temple of Minerva in Athens. The frontage of the main building is adorned by forty Doric columns. The sprawling compound of the Old Mint extends to nearly five hectares and includes seven other ancient structures including the Mint Master's house and the Mint warehouse buildings.

Encouragingly, the Heritage Conservation Committee of the Calcutta Municipal Corporation has recently approved proposals for an 'adaptive reuse project' for the Mint complex. Scheduled for completion in 2010, the emphasis will be on preserving the original structure of the heritage buildings on the site and adapting these to a mix of cultural and commercial use including a mint museum, print museum, archive centre, heritage hotel, an arts and crafts centre and retail outlets.

Continuing northwards along Strand Road, past the Old Mint and Nawab Lane on the right, you reach the next main junction, the eastern arm of which is Kali Krishna Tagore Street. This is the Posta Market area, a large and frenetic wholesale food bazaar. Here can be found mountains of vegetables and spices of every description. Be on the alert here for heavily laden coolies suddenly emerging at speed from the many narrow side lanes off this thoroughfare; it is far easier for you to avoid them than the other way around.

The fourth turning on the right eastwards along Kali Krishna Tagore Street and almost opposite the wonderfully named 'Good Luck Pharmacy' is the narrow Jogendra Kabira Row. This leads through to Kalkar Street which resembles a kind of open air warehouse, with so many goods randomly stacked in towering heaps on footpath and roadway. Moving south down Kalkar Street is something like an obstacle course but great fun nevertheless. This particular part of Burra Bazar was once known as Dhakapatti as it was home to the Sahas, cloth merchants from Dhaka in what is today Bangladesh.

Kalkar Street continues southwards a short way until it crosses Hari Ram Goenka Street which stretches both west and east of this point. Nearby are some prime examples of the horrendously jerry built and illegal over-development endemic throughout Burra Bazar and worthy of a short diversion. Do not be deterred by the maze of interlinking small lanes in this locality. If you should lose your bearings, anything west will lead you back out into Strand Road whilst anything east will take you out into Rabindra Sarani. Walking up the western arm of Hari Ram Goenka Street, the first turning on the right is an unnamed narrow lane next to numbers 58/59. This lane once led north to emerge at numbers 14/15 Bysack Street. As a result of illegal extensions to both sets of properties this lane is now all but blocked, even to pedestrians. Behind the eastern arm of Hari Ram Goenka Street is Shiv Thakur Lane (accessed via Goenka Lane or Sibtala Street, one turning east of the Kalkar Street crossing). Here at number 6 is a dilapidated, century old, building of five storeys that has been illegally extended vertically. The roadway in front of this building is less than two metres in width. No doubt one day these buildings and the many like them throughout the area will simply collapse as a result of their faulty construction or be consumed in a fire which no fire tender will have any chance of reaching.

Retrace your steps back to the eastern arm of Hari Ram Goenka Street and continue walking eastwards to Rabindra Sarani. This may take some time not because of the distance involved which is not much more than a few hundred metres, but due to the many interesting diversions this crowded and vibrant bazaar street has to offer.

On reaching Rabindra Sarani, if you wish to return to your starting point, turn right and walk south, passing the Nakhoda Mosque on your left. The Canning Street/Rabindra Sarani crossing is the next main junction. Alternatively, to reach the nearest metro station, (M.G. Road), once you leave Hari Ram Goenka Street, cross Rabindra Sarani and straight ahead is the beginning of Muktaram Babu Street. Walk east down this street, passing the Marble Palace on your right, until you reach Chitteranjan Avenue. Turn right here and M.G. Road metro station is located about one hundred and fifty metres south.

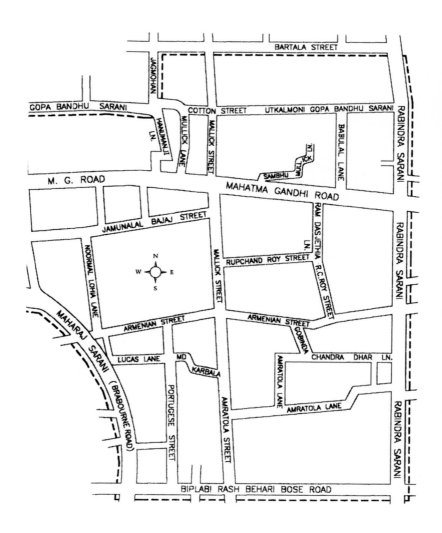

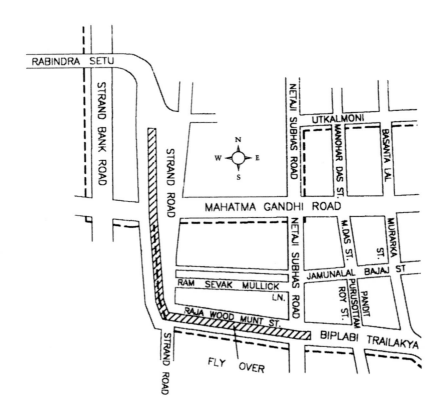

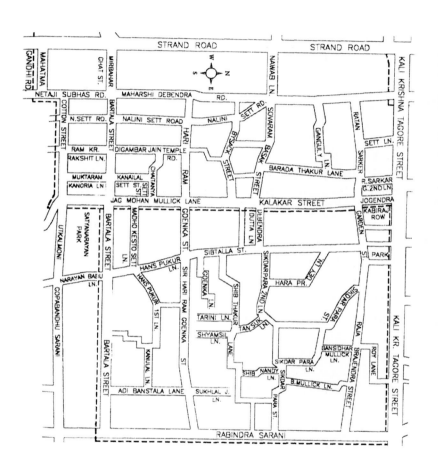

CHAPTER 4

Bagbazar, Sovabazar
and Shyambazar

This is the most northerly of the suggested walking tours and takes in the greater part of the three neighbouring areas of Bagbazar, Sovabazar (pronounced and sometimes spelt, Shobabazar) and Shyambazar. Together, these areas, traditionally regarded as the citadel of the Bengali aristocracy of Calcutta, are steeped in historical connection to a number of religious, cultural and philosophical movements. This walk takes in part of the area once known as Sutanuti where Job Charnock, finally set up a permanent trading base in 1690 (having had to flee the area on at least two previous occasions).

Both Bagbazar and Sovabazar have the River Hooghly as their western boundaries whilst Shyambazar, slightly to the east, straddles the northern extremities of Bidhan Sarani. The northern boundary of the area comprising these three neighbourhoods is the Circular Canal and the southern boundary, the old Grey Street, now renamed Sri Arabinda Sarani. The northern half of the area is served by Shyambazar metro station and the southern half by Sovabazar metro station.

A good starting point for this walk is, strange as it may seem, the Howrah Bridge. The first destination is to be Bagbazar Ghat and the most enjoyable way to get there is by river ferry. On reaching the Howrah side of the bridge, turn left and, keeping parallel with the river, walk through the ramshackle collection of hawkers' and small scale caterers' stalls. After a few hundred metres you come to the entrance to the bathing ghat, almost next door is the ticket office and entry to the ferry ghat. In the ticket office there are several small barred cubby holes from which to purchase your ticket. Make sure you go to the right one as each deals with a different set of destinations, identified in faded lettering just above eye level. If you get it wrong, the formidable Bengali ladies who dispense the tickets will soon put you right. A one way ticket to Bagbazar Ghat will be all of four rupees and fifty paise. Hang on to your ticket as you may be asked to produce it en route or when docking at your destination.

The ferry trip takes about twenty five minutes or so, including the two stops en route, first at Ahriatola Ghat then Sovabazar Ghat. This gives you enough time to take in the sights and your fellow passengers. You will almost certainly be the only westerner aboard that week, or month, and therefore the subject of much good natured curiosity. You will also find aboard a coterie of itinerant small traders and service providers. There will be the seller of nuts and other small snacks, the shoe clean man with his wooden box of brushes and polish and, often, an ear cleaning practitioner with his small wallet of gruesome looking instruments with which he removes wax from the ears of his clients.

Heading north up the Hooghly, most of the activity will be taking place on the eastern bank. After Ahriatola Ghat you will pass a number of bathing ghats and both the Nimtala and Kashi Mitra Burning Ghats. Bagbazar Ghat is the last stop on the route; the ferry waits here for fresh passengers before returning to Howrah Ghat. At the top of the ferry ramp, turn left and about one hundred metres on is a level crossing of the circular railway track. This is next to Bagbazar railway station which can be seen clearly a further fifty metres north. Before crossing the tracks have a look over the parapet wall to the river bank, where you should see, to your right, something which looks like one, sometimes two, giant floating haystacks. This is Bichali Ghat and the haystacks are country boats carrying paddy, so much of it that you can see no trace of the boat itself. How the boats still float under such mountains of cargo is little short of miraculous.

Once you have crossed the railway track a short walk east brings you to the junction with Rabindra Sarani; this far north not much more than a lane. Straight across the junction is the start of Bagbazar Street.; the main east/west artery through this area. The name Bagbazar is derived from the Bengali 'bagh' meaning flower garden and 'bazar' meaning market. As you walk east you pass, to your left the Bagbazar Durga Puja Ground. It is here that one of the oldest Durga festivals in all Calcutta is held.

Near to here, and no one now seems quite sure of the exact location, stood Perrin's Redoubt. This was a small, square fortification, a defensive outpost remote from the British stronghold at the old Fort William several miles to the south. Here on 16th June 1756, Ensign Francis Piccard, his sergeant, Peter Carey, a volunteer, Ralph Thoresby and 22 Dutch and Portuguese mercenaries, successfully resisted repeated attacks by a 4,000 strong force from the army of the Nawab of Bengal, Siraj-ud-Daula. Supported by the cannon of the East India Company ship 'St. George', moored in the Hooghly, and a relief force with further canon sent out from Fort William later in the day, the defenders of the Redoubt inflicted savage losses on the Nawab's troops, with 800 reported as being killed against British losses of 5. The Nawab's troops finally withdrew without taking the Redoubt. This heroic stand did not however, alter the overall outcome, as four days later the Nawab's troops overran the British at the old Fort William and captured Calcutta.

The ground to the front of the Redoubt had once been known as Perrin's Garden, Calcutta's most fashionable pleasure garden where 'it was the height of gentility for the (East India) Company's covenanted servants to take their ladies for an evening stroll or moonlight fete.' The Garden went into decline following the laying out of 'The Park' around Lal Dighi in front of old Fort William. The Garden was sold in 1752 and was later used as a site for the manufacture of gunpowder.

The rest of this part of Bagbazar Street, particularly the southern side, is taken up mainly by traders' stalls, tiny shops and eating places. The shopkeepers here take their security arrangements seriously. Count the number of padlocks on any of the shops which are closed and shuttered. I have found a few with as many as nine fist sized, padlocks employed.

At the end of this first part of Bagbazar Street turn left past Nivedita Park into N.K. Saha Lane. The third turning on your left is Udbodhan Lane (formerly known as Mukherjee Lane). Here at number 1 is the Ramakrishna Centre and Mission. This fine old building is also known as The Mother's House being once the home of Ma Sarada Devi 'The Holy Mother', wife and spiritual counterpart of Sri Ramakrishna, the great spiritual figure of 19th century India.

Continue north along N.K. Saha Lane, passing the Women's College on your left until the lane gives out onto the northern-most extremity of Rabindra Sarani and, to your right, the start of Galiff Street. Here in Galiff Street there is a weekly, Sunday market specialising in pet birds, goldfish, other animals and ornamental plants

Walking east along Galiff Street you pass the Chitpore Bridge on your left. This crosses the Circular Canal along whose banks, between this bridge and the Barrackpore Bridge further east, is often sited extensive illegal shanty settlements. These

are periodically cleared away but, inevitably, gradually reap-
pear; the poor and dispossessed having nowhere else to go. At
the height of the appalling Bengal famine in 1943[5] the banks all
along this Canal are said to have resembled a charnel house, so
great were the numbers of dead and dying, driven by starvation
to Calcutta from the hinterlands of Bengal.

After passing the Chitpore Bridge, take the first turning on the
right off Galiff Street. This is Nandalal Bose Lane which
contains some very fine and ancient residential buildings. About
half way along this Lane to your left is the start of Maratha
(sometimes spelt Mahratta) Ditch Lane; a reminder of that
ancient defensive work. The Ditch, designed to protect Calcutta
from attack from the landward side by the Maratha marauders,
ran for several kilometres from the Hooghly just north of
Bagbazar, all the way to the bottom end of present day
Chowringhee. It was excavated between 1740 and 1742 but
never fully completed. Somewhere very close to Maratha Ditch
Lane, part of the Ditch had been filled in to provide a rough
crossing called 'Cow Cross Bridge' which linked to the old track
eastwards to Dum Dum. The Ditch, through neglect of maintenance and failure to fully complete it, proved no defence at all
when the army of the Nawab of Bengal sacked Calcutta in
1756. The Ditch was finally filled in when, in 1799, construction of the old Circular Road commenced.

Almost opposite the beginning of Maratha Ditch Lane, on the
opposite side of Nandalal Bose Lane, is Thakur Radhakanta
Lane. This leads through to Haralal Mitra Lane containing a
number of interesting old residential buildings. Number 4 is
particularly significant with its grand front entranceway. A
short walk south along the Lane will bring you to the eastern
arm of Bagbazar Street. Turn left here then right into Girish
Avenue. Here, on the western pavement for a stretch of almost

[5]See Annexe 1 - Historical Notes

two hundred metres, is a line of appalling, illegal pavement shanties; hovels made up from bits of old brick, timber, scraps of tin, plastic sheeting and tarpaulin; of anything able to be scavenged locally. Mothers and elder daughters are squatting all over the pavement cooking over open fires or furiously thrashing laundry against the kerbstones, whilst dozens of small children in various stages of nakedness are happily playing amongst them. Near each shanty is a pile of salvaged plastic bottles and other recyclable rubbish which each family has scavenged and will sell on as a means of eking out a precarious living. I once saw here a whole group of children collecting tiny scraps of material, waste from around the local garment workshops, which their parents then rinsed, dried and, when enough had been accumulated, bundled up for sale.

Strangely, this is not the desolate scene that mere description would suggest. The people, mainly Biharis, seem to function well both as families and as part of their own micro community and, at least outwardly, appear good natured and cheerful. To my certain knowledge this particular settlement has been here for at least three years and has expanded considerably since I first came upon it. Any traveller from the west who may by now have been thinking his or her Calcutta lodgings rather lacking in accustomed comforts would do well to ponder on what these people would make of such accommodation.

Just past this settlement and occupying an incongruous position in the middle of the carriageway of Girish Avenue, is an intriguing old building. This is all that remains of the house of Girish Chandra Ghosh (1844-1912), from whom the Avenue takes its name. An accomplished Bengali musician, poet, playwright and novelist, he is said to have been a notorious libertine as a young man. In later life he was greatly influenced by the teachings of Sri Ramakrishna and became one of his closest disciples. When Girish Avenue was laid out in the early 1930's most of the Ghosh house had to be demolished; the portion remaining is all that could be spared.

Almost opposite the remains of the Ghosh house, on the eastern side of Girish Avenue, is the beginning of Ma Saradamoni Lane which has arms leading east, north and south of this point. This ancient and historic thoroughfare was once known as Bosepara Lane and contains some fine residential buildings, including the ancestral home of the distinguished and renowned Bose family at number 47B. It is known that Sri Ramakrishna first visited this house in 1877, a visit commemorated by a plaque there, in the Bengali script. Thereafter, the house became a regular meeting place for the great seer and his disciples.

It was also in Bosepara Lane where Sister Nivedita lived and there started her school for girls in 1898. Sister Nivedita, born Margaret Elizabeth Noble, was an Anglo Irish social pioneer, author and teacher who became a disciple of Swami Vivekananda. He gave her the name Nivedita which means one dedicated to God. She worked to improve the life of women of all castes and in later life embraced the cause of Indian nationalism. The school continues to this day but in different premises located in Nivedita Lane which can be found close by, off the western side of Girish Avenue.

Walking eastwards along the west/east arm of Ma Saradmoni Lane you will join Sachin Mitra Lane, another of Bagbazar's ancient residential thoroughfares. Seek out number 16 and you will find just to the side of this building the start of Biswakosh Lane. Once called Kantapukur By-Lane, this was where, at number 8, Nagendranath Basu (1866-1938) worked for more than twenty years to edit the 22 volume 'Biswakosh,' the Bengali encyclopaedia.

At the northern end of Sachin Mitra Lane you return to the eastern arm of Bagbazar Street. Turn right here and walk east for about 150 metres until you come to Bidhan Sarani (the old Cornwallis Street). Turning south, a short walk brings you to the madly busy Five Point Crossing; so called as it forms the convergence of five major thoroughfares, Bidhan Sarani, to the north and south, Bhupen Bose Avenue to the west, R.G. Kar Road to the east and Acharya Prafulla Chandra (A.P.C.) Road to the south east. This is the heart of Shyambazar.

Set in spectacular prominence in the centre of the crossing is the mounted statue of Subhas Chandra Bose, or 'Netaji', meaning, literally, respected leader and one of India's national heroes. He was one of the most prominent leaders of the Indian independence movement but disagreed strongly with Ghandi's tactics of non-violence and instead advocated violent resistance to British rule. Having seen the inside of numerous British Indian jails, he was exiled to Europe on the outbreak of war in 1939. His collaboration with the wartime German and Japanese Governments and later formation of the Indian National Army to fight against the British and their allies, are still matters of great controversy. He is supposed to have died when the airplane in which he was travelling to Japan crashed in Taiwan in August, 1945. This has never been proven conclusively and this doubt as to his actual fate has given rise to numerous conspiracy theories.

The Shyambazar Market can be found on the north western side of the crossing occupying the corner formed by Bidhan Sarani and R.G. Kar Road. The true scale of this market is not immediately apparent as much of the trading areas are tucked away under cover and entered via narrow walkways from the back edge of the pavement. This is not always so easy since most of the footpaths are taken up by hawkers and their wares. So bad has this congestion become in the past that the Calcutta Municipal Corporation has imposed restrictions here and in other streets across the City requiring that at least one third of pavements must be kept clear for pedestrians. Enforcing this is a different matter.

In Shyambazar Market, following the pattern of many Calcutta markets, clothing and general goods occupy the market perimeters with foodstuffs being concentrated towards the centre. Notice how the fruit and vegetable traders, when selling by weight, will produce ancient hand held scales; the produce one side balanced by crude iron weights the other side. The traveller from the west will ponder, with some amusement, just what their home grown weights and measures inspectors would make of this. Certainly the eagle-eyed purchasers seem quite satisfied they are not being short changed and one gets the impression that they would not be reticent in voicing any such objections. There is a large fish and meat section right at the centre of the market; a little slippery under foot and definitely not for the squeamish.

The Five Point Crossing is also the location of the Shyam-bazar metro station, with entrances to be found at various points around the junction. You will also find nearby the Tala Tank. Built in 1911, the Tank stands on a platform 30 metres high and has a capacity of approximately four million litres.

Leaving the Five Point Crossing via the southern arm of Bidhan Sarani, continue south and take the fourth turning on your right into Shyampuker Street. This is a good place to take a short diversion before continuing your route onwards to the Sovabazar area. The fourth turning on your right along Shyam-puker Street is the ancient Teliapara Lane. Look out for the lovely old cast iron street nameplate which uses the archaic spelling 'Talee Para Lane'. The Lane is a welcome, peaceful backwater after the hubbub of your recent surroundings, and contains a number of fine old residential buildings. One, a corner property, sports stone elephant heads, their raised trunks acting as supports for a first floor balcony. Some of the other buildings along the Lane have particularly fine detailing to the balconies.

At the eastern end of Teliapara Lane you join Ramdhan Mitra Lane. Running parallel to this and linked by a number of tiny unnamed by-lanes is Ramdhan Mitra By-Lane. It is worthwhile spending a little time exploring these byways which will reinforce any view you may have already formed that much of older parts of residential north Calcutta seem caught in a kind of pleasing time-warp with seemingly little changed since the early years of the 20th century. Keep walking north on any of these byways and you will emerge into Balaram Ghosh Street which runs between Bidhan Sarani to the east and Shyambazar Street to the west. Here you will find The Duff High School for Girls, another legacy to Calcutta of the Rev. Alexander Duff (1806-1878), a Scottish Presbyterian missionary credited as the founder of the Free Church of Scotland. He came to Calcutta in 1830 and stayed until 1863. During this time he was influential in the development of educational and social policy and was active in the founding of the first University of Calcutta. Until he left India, he was also President of the Bethune Society, a learned institution promoting the spirit of inquiry and knowledge amongst Bengalis. He edited the renowned 'Calcutta Review' from 1845 until 1849. His name will crop up time and again as the traveller becomes more familiar with the City's heritage.

Walking west along Balaram Ghosh Street you pass, on your left, the Shyampuker Police Station and a few metres further on, join the long, curving Shyambazar Street. Turn left here and head westwards, crossing the busy Jatindra Mohan Avenue (which marks your arrival at the Sovabazar area), until you come out into Raja Naba Krishna Street, very close to the junction with Rabindra Sarani. The Sovabazar Market lies just south of this point, sprawling either side of Rabindra Sarani. This busy market is mainly under cover and has the usual layout with foodstuffs towards the centre and clothing and general goods traded around the perimeter. You can find here particularly impressive displays of fruit and vegetables and rather less appealing, (at least to delicate western sensitivities), displays of fish and poultry, the latter being very much still alive immediately prior to purchase.

Leaving the market, by any exit, you can easily retrace your way back to Rabindra Sarani. Then, walking northwards you pass, on your left, Abhoy Mitra Lane. After this junction, take the next turning on your left which is Banamali Sarkar Street. This is the neighbourhood of Kumartuli, well known for its workshops of image makers and potters (Kumors). These craftsmen are renowned for their skill in constructing larger than life earthenware and clay images of the Hindu deities, particularly the goddesses Durga and Kali. These workshops are particularly busy from September to October, in preparation for the forthcoming Festivals. Then you will see armies of these images, in various stages of construction, left lined up outside the workshops to solidify in the sun before being painted.

At the western end of Banamali Sarkar Street you meet the tracks of the Circular Railway. Crossing the tracks brings you into Strand Bank Road directly opposite the Champatola Ghat. A short distance south along Strand Bank Road you come to Sovabazar Ghat from where you can catch a ferry to return to Howrah Ghat and your starting point. Before doing this, spend a little time exploring Sovabazar Street which begins back across the railway tracks, opposite the ferry ghat.

As you walk east along Sovabazar Street you again get that feeling of being transported back to an earlier era. The first part, (western end), of the Street is lined with the frontages of ancient godowns and workshops that look as if they have not been touched since the day they were constructed, probably in the last quarter of the 19th century. The Street, further east, hosts a kind of informal market with pavement traders selling mainly foodstuffs, including fish. On the southern side of the Street, at number 92B, you will find a very surprising building. This is the

Batakrishna Dham, the ancestral home of Butto Kristo Paul, the founder of a multi-national pharmaceutical firm and a close associate of and benefactor to the Ramakrishna Mission. The building is possibly best described as executed in a kind of wedding cake style with a profusion of eastern embellishments added: architecturally eccentric maybe but nevertheless very pleasing.

Sovabazar Street ends a little further east where it meets Rabindra Sarani. If, rather than return by river ferry, the metro is a better option, Sovabazar metro station can be found about one hundred metres along Sri Arabinda Sarani which begins directly opposite, on the other side of Rabindra Sarani.

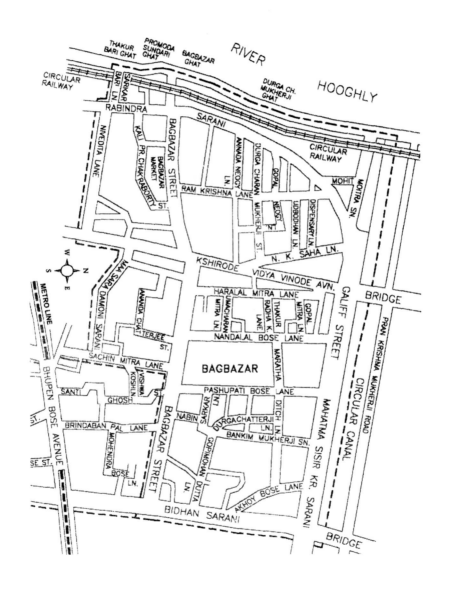

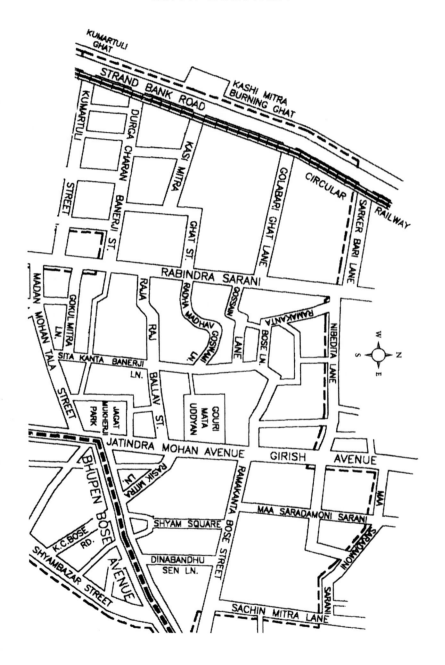

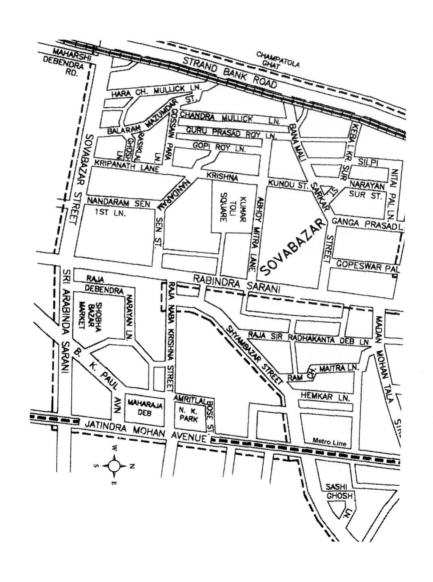

CHAPTER 5

Jorasanko (North) and Chor Bagan

This walk takes in those parts of the Jorasanko and Chor Bagan areas which straddle Chitteranjan Avenue between Mahatma Ghandi (M.G.) Road in the south, Vivekananda Road to the north and with Bidhan Sarani and Rabindra Sarani forming the eastern and western boundaries respectively. These areas are served by both M.G. Road and Girish Park metro stations.

Whilst there seems to be no clear demarcation between the respective boundaries of these two areas, for our purposes Jorasanko may be regarded at occupying the area west of Chitteranjan Avenue with Chor Bagan occupying the area to the east.

Jorasanko is said to take its name from two (jora) ancient wooden bridges (sanko) which once spanned a stream in this locality. Records have shown the area to have been known by this name at least as early as the 1780's when it appears in the list of Calcutta's thanas (police stations) compiled at that time. It is famous, amongst other things for being the ancestral home of the distinguished Tagore family. The origins of Chor Bagan, meaning, literally thieves' garden, are equally ancient but less clear

The now familiar M.G. Road/Chitteranjan Avenue crossing again provides a convenient starting point. Setting out from the north western corner of the crossing, walk west along M.G.

Road and take the second turning on your right into Ram Lochan Mullick Street. Here all your senses are immediately assailed by the sights, sounds, smells and general frenzy of activity which suddenly envelopes you; for you have entered the Mechua Fruit Market.

This wholesale Market is the largest of its kind in the City, and very possibly within all of West Bengal. The Market sprawls northwards along Ram Lochan Mullick Street crosses Madan Mohan Burman Street and continues along the whole length of Balmukund Makkar Road right to its junction with Chitteranjan Avenue; a distance of some several hundred metres. Walking the market streets, which are carpeted in straw, you are dwarfed by gigantic piles of fruit of every description. Mountains of bananas piled to first storey level, huge pyramids of pineapples, melons, pomegranates, jackfruit, papaya and whatever else is in season. When the various varieties of mango start to arrive, upwards of 800 tons of this fruit alone are traded here daily. Weaving skilfully amongst all this are the market coolies balancing on their heads huge baskets and stacked boxes of produce or enormous stems of bananas. Witnessing the sheer strength and sense of balance displayed in their work can be a humbling experience.

Once you cross Madan Mohan Burman Street into Balmukund Makkar Road, the hustle and bustle of the market actually increases. Here you will see the auctioneers and prospective purchasers in voluble action as they haggle over prices and quantities. Standing by patiently are the coolies ready to rush off with their loads to the successful bidder's transport. These auctions must be a popular spectator pastime for there seems to be, for every one person actively engaged in the business of the market, at least ten lookers on, you being one of them.

The eastern end of Balmukund Makkar Road joins Chitteranjan Avenue just north of the M.G. Road metro station. Cross the Avenue at this point and less than fifty metres south you come to Mahajati Sadan. This fine and impressive building is not actually as old as the architectural style may suggest. The foundation stone was laid in 1939 but construction was suspended for the duration of the Second World War. Work finally recommenced following independence and the building was completed in 1958. The building, which has the status of National Institution, contains a huge auditorium where programmes of various cultural organisations and anniversary celebrations of the great and the good, are regularly staged.

The first turning on the left past Mahajati Sadan is the eastern arm of Madan Mohan Burman Street which stands in stark contrast to its grand neighbour. The first part of the Street usually has a collection of makeshift pavement shanties occupied by rag pickers whose stock lies all over the place in unruly heaps. This Street was previously called Mechuabazar Street, a reminder of the ancient name by which this general area was once known. There is still a fragment of a Mechuabazar Lane, a little further east down near where the old College Street Market once stood.

Walking east, the first turning on the left is Mitra Lane where you can find some of the best tinsmiths in Calcutta. Along the whole 200 metre or so length of the Lane, you will encounter mountains of empty cooking oil tins, some new but most brought here for refurbishment or recycling. You will see handcarts and bicycle carts arriving and departing impossibly overloaded with these tins, all roped together in tottering, unstable piles, threatening to overspill onto the roadway with every change of direction.

There are numerous small, open fronted workshops hereabouts occupied by tinsmiths squatting by old fashioned soldering irons heating over open charcoal fires. To watch these men work is an education. One continuous and quick swipe with the soldering iron is all they need to secure a bottom or a top to the body of a new can. They are a friendly lot who will even let you try out your skill with the soldering iron if you show sufficient interest.

Just before you reach the northern end of Mitra Lane, there is a small unnamed by-lane off to your right. This will take you through to Muktaram Babu Lane which, less than 50 metres south, becomes Marcus Square. The Square itself now has the official and universally ignored name of Charlie Chaplin Square and is a sort of walled and gated compound housing a large number of retail trading outlets. If you are in the market for some fine teas, then seek out the old established firm of Subodh Brothers who currently have an outlet here at number A30.

It is well worth walking around the outside perimeter of Marcus Square if for no other reason than to gain some understanding of the amount of recycling which takes place in this City. Here are the 'transit depots' to which the local rag pickers and scavengers after plastic bottles, cardboard and paper bring their loaded sacks. This has been going on since long before anyone had ever heard of climate change or global warming and whilst the primary motivation is one of economic necessity rather than some altruistic concern for the future of the planet, the end result is the same. Go out into Chitteranjan Avenue which is one of those main thoroughfares where litter bins are provided every few hundred metres along its length. These bins are certainly used heavily but you will be lucky to find anything in them, for all that is salvageable has been removed almost immediately it has been deposited. You can stand and see this happening. This certainly contrasts very favourably with the wasteful, throwaway nature of many western societies. It is perhaps something that those, mainly western, environmental evangelists would do well to bear in mind before sanctimoniously lecturing countries like India on their high carbon footprint.

Having completed your clockwise circuit of the Square you find yourself back in Madan Mohan Burman Street. Heading east, the next turning on your left is Balak Dutta Lane. This long, narrow and busy thoroughfare is home to many a metal bashing enterprise. Here you will find the battered and beyond repair cooking oil tins, the rejects of Mitra Lane so to speak, being brutally flattened out, bundled up and destined for the scrap metal yards and eventual recycling. Continuing northwards along the Lane it becomes increasingly congested so that it is difficult to be sure you are still on the footpath and not walking through someone's living space. No one seems to mind and you rather get the feeling that your presence is providing a mildly interesting diversion to the locals.

It was along Balak Dutta Lane that I once encountered a group of five Hijiras, the eunuchs who live on the fringes of Indian Society and are either exotic oddities or damn nuisances, depending on your point of view. The group, all shod in high heels, extravagantly made up and robed in garish saris, told me that they had just come from a wedding where they had been paid to sing and dance. The truth was more likely to have been that they had been paid to go away, since their public embarrassment potential is one of their money making rackets; another, for some, is prostitution. One of their favourite and most lucrative scams is to attend outside the houses of families blessed with a new son or daughter, making such a spectacle and nuisance of themselves that the families bribe them generously to go away.

There are an estimated seven hundred thousand Hijira in India, mostly based in the larger cities and towns where they live in tight knit and well organised communities under recognised leaders. Some, a minority, can appear amazingly convincing as females, others could not be less so, many sporting a three or four day stubble on their chins. This particular band were all quite feminine, responding girlishly to my respectfully favourable comments as to their appearance and dress.

At the northern end of Balak Dutta Lane you join Muktaram Babu Street. This Street links Bidhan Sarani to the east with Rabindra Sarani to the west, crossing Chitteranjan Avenue about half way along its length. Turning left into Muktaram Babu Street, cross to the northern pavement and walking westwards past the Goenka Hospital take the second turning on your right into Amar Bose Sarani. From here on you enter an area of ancient narrow lanes many retaining their fine, original cast iron nameplates, some in archaic spelling. There is a small maze of such lanes to be found just west of Amar Bose Sarani and accessed via tiny by-lanes located at the first and second turnings on your left. Should you lose direction whilst navigating these lanes, simply strike out south along any of them and you will rejoin Muktaram Babu Street just to the west of the junction with Amar Bose Sarani.

Here, as in numerous other locations throughout north Calcutta, I have often been approached by helpful locals enquiring if I needed help or directions. So few western travellers venture into these parts that they find it surprising that you have come by design rather than by accident and they generally seem rather pleased when they learn that you have.

Further north along Amar Bose Sarani, this thoroughfare becomes Chor Bagan Lane, a reminder of the area's ancient and possibly murky, past character. About half way along the Lane, there stands an ancient Banyan Tree which could most likely shed light on the old rumours about this area, if only it had the power of speech.

Chor Bagan Lane ends where it meets Tarak Pramanick Road. Turning left and heading westwards along this curving Road you quickly reach Chitteranjan Avenue, just south of the Girish Park crossing. Almost opposite, across the Avenue, is the beginning of Baranasi Ghose Lane. This serpentine lane contains some fine old residential mansions, mostly of 19th century

construction. Heading westward along the lane, the second
turning on the left is Rajendra Mullick Lane, named after Raja
Rajendra Mullick who built the Marble Palace. As you turn left
and head south down this Lane you can just catch a distant
glimpse of this magnificent structure. A visit there is included in
this walk but by a slightly less direct route.

Passing Baranasi Ghosh 2nd and 3rd Lanes on your right, the
first crossing you come to is Madan Chatterjee Lane. Turn right
here and walk westwards towards Rabindra Sarani. To your
right, behind the buildings fronting the Lane, is the Jorasanko
Thakur Bari, the ancestral home of the distinguished Tagore
family. Now the Rabindra Bharati University, it can be accessed
via Dwarkanath Tagore Lane, the last turning on your right off
Madan Chatterjee Lane, or from the main gateway located in
Rabindra Sarani. This fine heritage building was built by
Dwarkanath Tagore (the grandfather of the Nobel Literature
Laureate, Rabindranath Tagore), in the late 18th century and
has since been sympathetically restored. It also houses the
Tagore Museum detailing the history of the family and its influential role in the 19th century Bengali religious and cultural
renaissance. The Museum is open between 10.00 am and 5.00
pm on weekdays and to 1.30 pm on Saturdays. There is also an
excellent light and sound show staged, in English, on weekdays
commencing 7.00 pm (November to January) and commencing
8.00 pm (February to June). Well worth attending.

Still in Madan Chatterjee Lane, just past the entrance to
Dwarkanath Tagore Lane but on the other side of the thoroughfare, you will find the wonderfully named Panchi Dhopani
Gullee. At the end of the Gullee, turn right into the equally
wonderfully named Doodwala Dharmashala Lane. This Lane
performs a ninety degree turn to the right before joining the
western arm of Muktarum Babu Street. Here, at number 46, set
back from the Street amidst beautiful gardens and behind classical iron railings and gates, is the Marble Palace. Just about the

most unlikely building you would ever expect to encounter here. Given the uniqueness and size of the Palace, it has always struck me as odd that those who decide such matters perceived a need to identify it further by allocating to it a street number. I am rather glad that they did.

Built in the Neoclassical style by Raja Rajendra Mullick between 1835 and 1840, this graceful mansion takes its name from the fine marble panelled walls and floors of its interior. Looking from the gateway across the gardens, complete with Italianate fountain and statuary, to the Palace's Palladian frontage, it is difficult to believe that you are still in Calcutta and have not somehow been transported magically to some quiet corner of, say, Rome or Florence.

Within, the Palace is even more surprising. You would be forgiven for thinking it to be a madly overstocked museum; which it is not. The Palace is still the family home of the Mullicks and the enormous collections of sculpture, furniture, clocks, mirrors, chandeliers, paintings, porcelain, pottery and glassware are all objects collected over the years by generations of the family on its frequent travels around the globe.

The Palace is open to visitors every day except Tuesdays and Thursdays between 10.00 am and 4.00 pm. However, it is necessary first to obtain a ticket, at least one day in advance of your proposed visit, from the Government of India Tourist Office located at 4 Shakespeare Sarani, just off the southern end of Chowringhee, (Maidan being the nearest metro station).

On leaving the Marble Palace turn right and walk eastwards along Muktaram Babu Street to Chitteranjan Avenue. Cross to the other side of the Avenue from where you can get a good view of the start of the western arm of Muktarum Babu Street, which you have just left and of Madan Chatterjee Lane, the next turning northwards. Just to the right of the former is a tall, white building. This fabulously ornate structure, rising through five storeys, is Gopal Bhawan, built in 1927 but in a style belonging to a much earlier age. Gracing the entrance to the latter is a huge and ornate archway surmounted with a large bust of Rabindranath Tagore, marking the entrance to the eastern approach to the Jorasanko Thakur Bari.

Your starting point is just a short distance south along Chitteranjan Avenue. On your way there, you will pass the M.G. Road metro station.

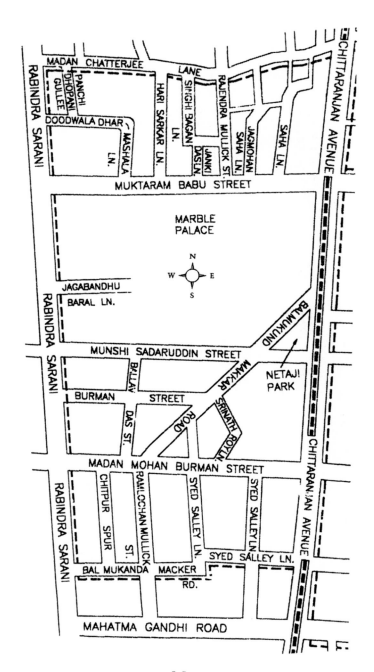

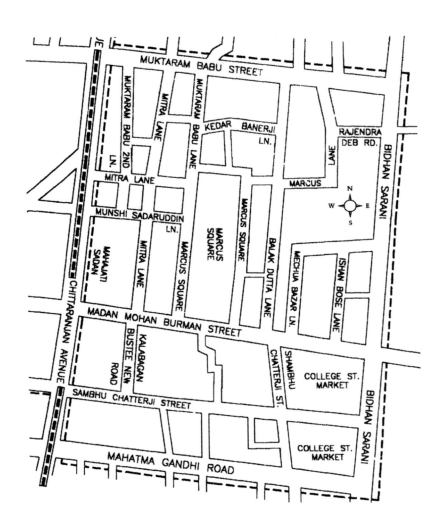

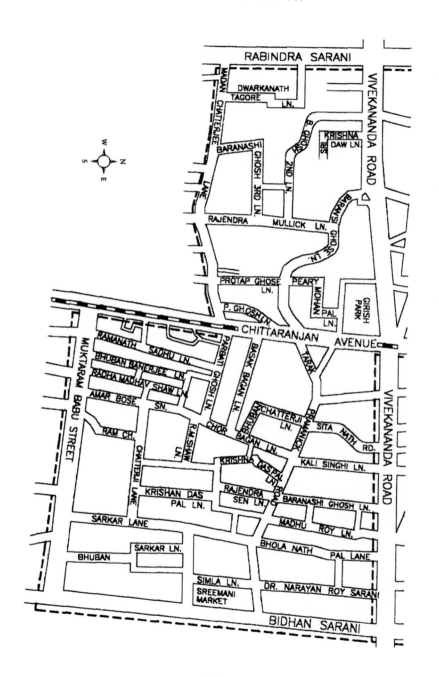

CHAPTER 6

Amherst Street (South) to Sealdah and Muchipara (North)

This walk takes in the area around the eastern reaches of Mahatma Ghandi (M.G.) Road, beyond College Street, and towards Sealdah. It also explores the eastern parts of the Bow Bazar area known as Muchipara (north). The nearest metro stations serving these areas are M.G. Road and Central, although both stations are located on the western extremities of the areas here covered.

The junction of M.G. Road and College Street provides as good a starting point as any. This is only a short walk east of the now familiar M.G. Road/Chitteranjan Avenue crossing.

Before heading off from this crossing, spend a little time watching how the traffic negotiates this hugely busy junction, helped or hindered, depending on your point of view, by the sequence of the traffic signals, reinforced by the commands of the duty traffic policemen. Both the Chitteranjan Avenue and M.G. Road approaches to this junction are straight and wide enough for the traffic to get up a fair lick of speed. Indeed, there is every incentive for it to do so since, to be caught by the traffic signals can involve a delay of several minutes. The result is that the less rule orientated drivers cannot always bring their vehicles to a halt as quickly as the signals require. This, coupled with the frantic jostling for position in the ranks of the halted vehicles anxious to speed off the second the signals allow, and you have a kind of continuous battle for life being enacted throughout the more congested periods, which in these parts of Calcutta is often from early morning until well after dark. This is made all the more dramatic by the universal habit of halted vehicles, from heavy lorries to motor cycles, having their engines switched off whilst awaiting the signal to move off. Once that comes, there is the roar of many scores of engines being restarted and revved in unison. This is the signal for any pedestrians unlucky enough to be still on the highway, to dive for the footpath before they are engulfed by the whole tidal wave of two and three wheelers, taxis, cars, buses, lorries, trams and assorted porters on foot or under pedal power.

From the College Street/M.G. Road junction, walk east along the latter and take the first turning on the left. This is Tamer Lane, a relatively quiet backwater containing some interesting large residential buildings dating from the 19th century. One of these buildings, precisely which is not recorded, once housed a private club said to be famous for its accomplished bagpipe band. The far end of this Lane joins Beniatola Lane where, turning right you rejoin M.G. Road.

A few hundred metres further east is the junction with Amherst Street. Now officially renamed Ram Mohan Roy Sarani, it is one of those thoroughfares where the dual use of the old and new names still persists. Amherst Street was one of the early main thoroughfares in Calcutta. Named after Lord (later Earl) Amherst, Governor General of the old East Company from 1824 until 1845, it links Manicktala Market at Vivekananda Road in the north with Bow Bazar at B.B Ganguly Street in the south. Turning left at this junction and walking northwards you pass, to your right, the Roman Catholic Holy Trinity Church. Almost next door is St. Paul's School, established in the 1830's, making it one of the oldest in Calcutta. On your left is the enormous, red brick Mawari

Hospital, looking as if built to last a thousand years and the strongest of sieges, so massive in design is its construction. The high external walls of the Hospital running along Amherst Street also provide support to scores of lean-to ramshackle pavement shanties. The population of this makeshift settlement, mainly economic refugees from the neighbouring States of Bihar and Orrisa, must number in the hundreds; I once counted upwards of sixty children here and they were just the ones visible out on the pavement.

It took me a long while to grasp that these seemingly haphazard collections of temporary hovels, constructed flimsily of anything readily to hand, are often reproductions in miniature of the rural villages from where many of these people originated, in some cases complete even with poultry and livestock. This, like so many such illegal settlements, will periodically be cleared away by the authorities, banishing the inhabitants to God knows where. But gradually it will start to re-form and the whole process will begin over again.

A little further north, Amherst Street crosses Keshab Sen Street. Turn right here and, walking eastwards, you will see much bathing at the numerous street standpipes to be found hereabouts. Very refreshing it looks too with the thermometer hovering around 38 degrees C.

There is also an abundance of rickshaws parked up all along this part of the Street, often in groups of as many as fifty at a time, all slotted together by their shafts. The reason is the presence in this locality of a number of 'depots' operated by rickshaw barons where rickshaws are garaged and repaired.

It was close by that I met Bappa Mahato, a rickshaw puller for almost twenty years. Originally from Bihar, Bappa, like most other rickshaw pullers, does not own the rickshaw he pulls; this is owned by one of the local rickshaw barons and rented out to him at a daily rate. His long day begins just after sunrise and seldom ends before dusk. On a good day he will earn about 200 Rupees, hauling his rickshaw a distance of between 15 to 20 kilometres through Calcutta's streets. A good part of his day is taken up with regular commissions: deliveries of newspapers to the various vendors dotted around the neighbourhood, ferrying children to and from school and supplies from the markets to local shops and houses. In between all this, he is always on the lookout for casual fares, tapping his bell on the shafts of his rickshaw to attract attention.

The hand pulled rickshaw, unique to and a symbol of Calcutta, may finally be heading for extinction. Originally introduced in the closing decade of the 19th century by Chinese shopkeepers to ferry goods around the City and since 1919 permitted to carry passengers, there are now an estimated 35,000 rickshaw pullers operating in the City. The State Government, back in 2005, decided that the hand pulled rickshaw was detrimental to the City's image and had to go. Now technically illegal, the hand pulled rickshaw is still very much in evidence throughout Calcutta and no doubt will remain so whilst debate rages backwards and forwards interminably about the prospects for re-training and finding alternative livelihoods for the tens of thousands economically dependent on this form of transport.

The second turning on your right along the Street is Baithakkhana Road. This Road, leading all the way south through to B.B. Ganguly Street, is a reminder of much earlier times. In the mid 18th century, the whole thoroughfare leading from Lal Bazar through to where Sealdah Railway Station now stands, roughly equating with present day B.B. Ganguly Street, was known by the name Baithakkhana. It took this name from an ancient Banyan Tree at the eastern extremity which formed a baithakkhana, or resting and meeting place for merchants and their caravans.

Immediately north of the Baithakkhana Road junction is a series of narrow, interconnecting and unnamed alleyways. These can be accessed from both the Road itself and also from Keshab Sen Street. The quarter of an hour or so necessary to explore these alleys is time well spent particularly since the locals, whose homes I was nosing around, struck me as an amiable lot who treated my unexpected presence amongst them as an amusing distraction.

Back on Keshab Sen Street, a further one hundred metres east brings you out onto Acharya Prafulla Chandra (A.P.C.) Road, the former (Upper) Circular Road. The busy junction at this location is known as Rajabazar Crossing; Rajabazar also being the name of the whole area south of here strung out along APC Road, as far as the beginning of the Sealdah Flyover.

Turning right at the Rajabazar Crossing and walking south you are treading the route of the old Maratha Ditch, that extensive but ultimately ineffective eastern line of defence for 18th century Calcutta. You will pass the Victoria Institution College to your right, a noted and respected educational establishment for women. Almost opposite the College on the other side of APC Road is the sprawling Rajabazar Tram Depot, a place of loud clanking, banging, grinding and other sounds of repair and maintenance, audible even above the roar of the traffic flowing between. For those interested in taking a closer look, the Depot, can be accessed by using the pedestrian overbridge sited a little further south. The alternative involves locating and squeezing through any convenient gap in the iron railings running down the middle of the carriageway, an option favoured only by local risk takers in a particular hurry.

There is a lot of pavement trading activity all along the Rajabazar stretch of APC Road. This intensifies once you pass the junction with Surya Sen Street on your right and come within sight of the Sealdah Flyover. There is a particular section which seems to specialise in worn out motor spares. Stripped down engines, gearboxes and other auto innards heaped about in piles all over the slippery, oil stained pavement along with headlamps, worn tyres, miscellaneous electrical components and patched up exhaust systems; all of which seem to have a ready market.

The Sealdah Flyover, statistically, said to be the busiest stretch of road anywhere in the City begins to rise here and is then joined from the right by the ramp from the eastern end of M.G. Road, before being carried over and beyond the B.B. Ganguly Street/Beliaghata Road crossing. Just to the right, along Manindra Nath Mitra Row, is Dim Patty, the City's wholesale egg market.

Much of the space beneath the Flyover is given over to a sprawling and very busy general retail market which also spills over onto all the adjoining pavements. You can buy just about anything here from brightly coloured plastic buckets to dried fish; shiny metal pots of every conceivable size to badges, posters and fridge magnets depicting Hindu deities. There is a large clothing section where you can pick up a wide variety of 'genuine' designer wear and accessories from the likes of Gucci, Armani and Hugo Boss for an absolute song. As with those gentlemen trading in 'genuine' Rolex watches, who are to be found at their stalls along Chowringhee, one has to wonder just how they do it for the price!

Located just before the junction with B.B. Ganguly Street are a group of traders who must have cornered the City's market in underpants. They have seemingly thousands of pairs of men's underpants on display; nothing else just this one commodity in every size, pattern and colour imaginable. Nearby, there are similar one commodity concerns dealing in such things as handkerchiefs, socks, shoelaces and padlocks. Here, as in similar markets throughout Calcutta nowadays there are growing numbers of outlets dealing in mobile phones, phone acces-sories, repairs and upgrades; a sure sign of India's advancing economy.

Dipping under the approximate centre of the Sealdah Flyover, is an underpass which leads to the approach to Sealdah Railway Station. Once through this underpass, with the Seal-dah Court complex just to your right, the main station en-trance lies straight ahead, just beyond the taxi rank. Sealdah is Calcutta's second main railway station, after Howrah. It is ac-tually two stations behind a single impressive frontage; one providing services to the suburbs and settlements surrounding the metropolis and the other serving more distant destinations in eastern India. To get some idea of the sheer scale of the services operating from this station, you need to visit during the morning or evening rush hours. Standing in the main concourse it is as if a sizeable chunk of Calcutta's population is on the move at the same time, departing and arriving in a constant stream, packing every train and platform to bursting point. Behind all this apparent chaos, there must be some very sound organisation employed to make it all work, and work it does to a degree that would put many a UK rail oper-ator to shame.

Returning through the underpass, the start of B.B. Ganguly Street lies straight ahead. It is somewhere near to this spot that popular legend has Job Charnock sitting smoking a hookah under a large Banyan Tree whilst conducting his trading on behalf of the East India Company. Precisely where this tree stood has been the subject of endless argument down the years. This tree was certainly shown on a 1794 map of Calcutta but, curiously, an earlier and more detailed map of 1784 made no mention of it. Some have it that the tree was cut down with the laying out of the Circular Road in the closing years of the 18th century, others hold that its demise was the building of the first Sealdah Railway Station, half a century later.

The first turning on your right along B.B. Ganguly Street is the southern end of Baithakkhana Road, the other end of which was encountered off Keshab Sen Street earlier in this walk. The Baithakkhana bazaar is to be found along this southern end of the Road and is a good place to shop for a wide variety of spices or just a visit to enjoy the pungent aromas.

It was down B.B. Ganguly Street (then called Bow Bazar Street), that Calcutta's first tram rolled out in February, 1873. This was a horse drawn affair running between Sealdah Railway Station and Armenian Ghat Street, via Bow Bazar and Dalhousie Square, a distance of approximately four kilometres. Unfortunately, the service attracted too few passengers and was wound up in November of the same year. It was reintroduced in 1880 following the formation of the Calcutta Tramways Company. Electric traction was not introduced to this and other tram routes in the City until the closing years of the 19th century. There is a full size replica of an original horse drawn tram, which doubles as a kind of knick-knack shop, at the affluent City Centre Arcade out at Salt Lake.

There are numerous ancient lanes leading off both the southern and northern sides of this stretch of B.B. Ganguly Street. This walk explores those on the northern side; those on the southern side being covered in a different walk detailed at Chapter 10. Many of these lanes once contained Kothas or Baiji-quarters, which housed numerous singing and dancing girls and their teachers and were the haunt of the cultured rich of Calcutta. The famous Kathak guru, Ram Narayan Mishra is known to have regularly taught in this area. The Kothas have been in decline for many years. Although some remain, they are now few in number.

The eastern end of the Street, between the Flyover and the junction with Amherst Street, houses the premises of many a wholesale trader in fruit and vegetables. There are enormous baskets of produce stacked all over the footpaths and along the road-way attended by an army of coolies. It is quite usual to see two or more of these remarkable men struggling to lift onto the head of a colleague, a huge basket weighing anything up to 100 kilos. Once loaded, off he moves at a pace it is difficult to keep up with, even encumbered with no more than a knapsack and water bottle.

As you draw nearer the junction with Amherst Street, take any of the small lanes to your right which will lead through to Lattoo Para Bustee, home to numerous poor Bihari families. Many of the heads of these families you will have just seen nearby engaged as coolies. Others will earn their living as sweepers, rickshaw or cycle-van wallas, some with a sideline in scaveng-ing and recycling anything saleable. A bustee is, essentially a collection of slum habitations but with the crucial difference that it has legal status; it is a registered slum, recognised by the Calcutta Municipal Corporation under an Act of 1980 which gave official definition to a bustee. The makeshift settlements of squatter shanties, flung up along canal banks, railway tracks beside garbage dumps and along pavements do not 'enjoy' the status of the registered bustee; they are essentially illegal encroachments and can be swept away at an hour's notice.

The Lattoo Para Bustee does at least enjoy some access to essential basic amenities such as water and rudimentary sanita-tion and the construction types of the habitations there would be classed as falling within the upper end of the Bustee struc-tural ratings scale (there truly does exist such a thing), which ranges from pukka (soundly constructed) to kutcha (crude). Nevertheless, living conditions here are poor but perhaps not so poor as those which forced the inhabitants' migration to the City in the first place.

In one of the shanties here I was able to see in operation one of the staple cottage industries of the Bustees; the manufacture of beedies. The beedie (or bidi) is the poor man's cigarette, a few strands of tobacco rolled in a kindu leaf and tied with cotton thread into bundles of 5 or 10 ready for sale. The task requires considerable dexterity and is therefore well suited to the nimble fingers of young children. One of the workers in this particular enterprise was Malabika, a pretty and engaging nine year old girl who lived with her family a few doors away. She did this work whenever she could be spared from other chores and even found time to attend a local primary school for one or two days per week.

Retracing your steps back onto B.B. Ganguly Street, at number 167 near the junction with Amherst Street and next door to the Bank of India, is Gupta's Restaurant. This well known establishment serves excellent lunchtime thalis and a range of excellently cooked traditional Bengali dishes in the evenings. Almost opposite, on the southern side of the Street is the Hotel Kolkata, rumoured to employ the rudest staff in the entire City.

From Gupta's, cross to the western pavement of Amherst Street and walking northwards, take the third turning on your left. This is Prem Chand Boral Street, one of the oldest and most active red light areas in Calcutta. One thing that needs to be understood about such areas in Calcutta is that they are rarely as seedy or intimidating as are their counterparts in many western cities. For a start, there is much more going on than merely the traditional trade of the red light district. Most of these areas are also residential neighbourhoods, with local residents carrying on their ordinary day to day activities. Children with satchels walking to and from their schools, boys playing cricket in the streets, housewives with baskets out shopping for vegetables, people coming to or from their places of work or taking meals at street food stalls; the co-existence of these different activities is quite remarkable. That accepted, this, and other areas like it, whilst perfectly safe to navigate during the day, are not recommended after dark, particularly if you are unfamiliar with the through routes and at risk of getting lost.

The upper (eastern) end of Prem Chand Boral Street is unremarkable save for a number of small carpentry workshops with the carpenters sitting or standing outside performing minor masterpieces in wood with a basic toolkit of saw, chisel and spokeshave. The Street then opens out into a kind of square complete with small Hindu Temple to one side and food stalls and fruit and vegetable sellers to the other. It is here that you begin to notice that, amidst the usual throng of a busy Calcutta street, there are numbers of ladies more extravagantly dressed, coiffured and painted than is customary. As you leave the square and continue along the lower (western) arm of the Street, the number of such ladies increases: seated or standing about gossiping in groups outside dilapidated looking premises. I have always found them to be a cheerful and friendly lot. In my longer stays in Calcutta, I regularly use Prem Chand Boral Street as a convenient short cut from Sealdah Station out into College Street and on to Chitteranjan Avenue. As a consequence of being a frequent passer-by I came to be on nodding terms with a number of these ladies who would good naturedly rib me with extravagant invitations to sinful connection in their rooms and who would howl with laughter when, politely I declined, excusing myself on the grounds of advancing age.

Prem Chand Boral Street ends where it meets College Street. Turning right here and walking north past the book stalls, brings you back to your starting point at the junction with M.G. Road. Alternatively, on leaving Prem Chand Boral Street, cross College Road and take Eden Hospital Road (almost opposite), which, a few hundred metres on, meets Chitteranjan Avenue. Central metro station can be found another 75 metres south along the Avenue.

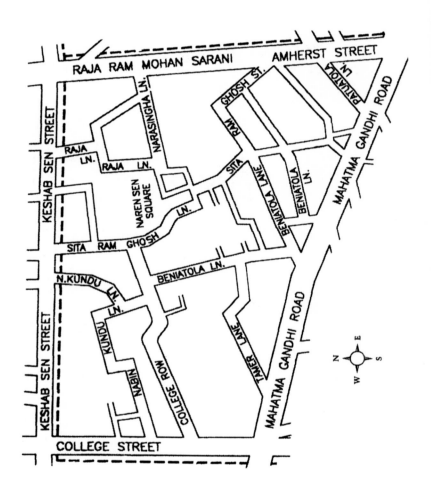

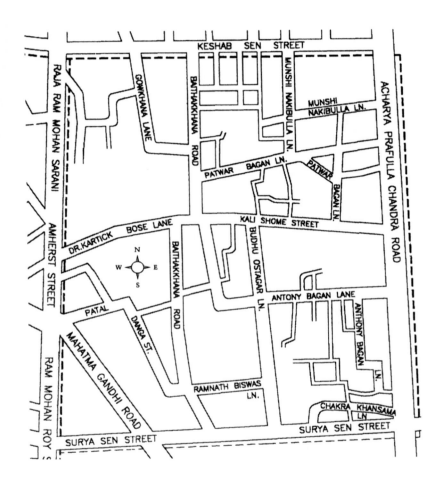

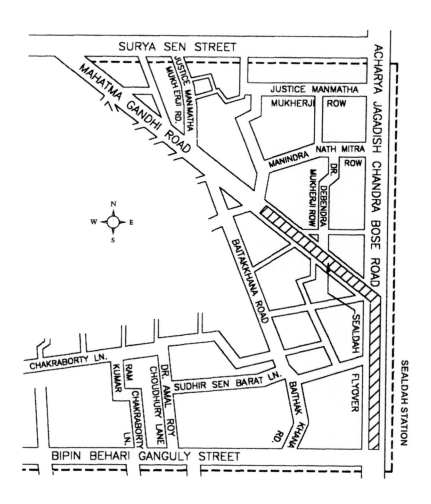

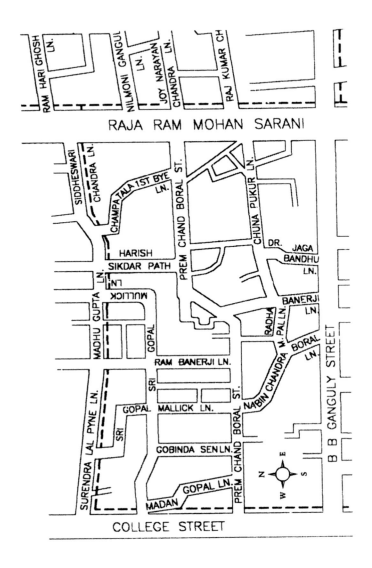

CHAPTER 7

Girish Park and Jorabagan (South)

This walk covers those parts of Girish Park and Jorabagan which lie between Vivekananda Road and Kali Krishna Tagore Street in the south and Beadon Street and Nimtala Ghat Street to the north. Bidhan Sarani and the Hooghly form the eastern and western boundaries respectively. For our purposes, Rabindra Sarani can be regarded as forming the dividing line between these two areas. Both areas are served by Girish Park metro station which provides a convenient starting point for this walk.

Girish Park, is named after Girish Chandra Ghose the famous Bengali poet, playwright and musician, whose home (or at least the remaining part of it) still survives further north in Girish Avenue and was visited in the walk described in Chapter 4. Girish Park, adjacent to the metro station of the same name, contains his statue.

Jorabagan means 'two gardens' and is so named because a road through it led out to two garden houses owned by Gobindram Mitter and Umichand, two rather shadowy but enormously influential characters who merit further scrutiny.

Gobindram Mitter (also spelled Mitra) was one of the first Indian officials under the East India Company's Presidency of Calcutta. He first came on the scene in the early years of the

18th century and was later to earn notoriety for his tyranny, wealth and extravagance.

He was appointed in 1720 as Deputy Collector (or Black Zemindar as the title then ran), to assist the Company's English Collector in the task of gathering rents and taxes. The position also carried certain judicial and municipal responsibilities. Although answerable, via the Collector and Governor General, to the Presidency's Council, it is clear that, in practical terms the real day to day power was wielded by the Deputy. In this post, which he held until 1756, Gobindram Mitter became a legend in his own lifetime, amassing enormous personal wealth, achieved through both fair means and foul. He built a huge residence in Kumortuli in grounds of 7 hectares as well as a garden villa where he housed his favourite mistresses. In 1731 he built a magnificent nine turreted temple near Kurmortuli, the loftiest pinnacle of which is said to have been even higher than the 50 metre tall Ochterlony Monument (present day Saheed Minar). This temple was, apparently, destroyed in the earthquake and cyclone of 1737.

There seems to have been some official disquiet about the power wielded by the 'Black Zemindar' and his methods. John Zephaniah Holwell, the Presidency's Collector from 1752 until 1756, (and later survivor of the 'Black Hole' and subsequently Governor General) wrote of his Deputy, 'a power of perpetuity devolved on the standing deputy, who was always styled the 'Black Zemindar' and such was the tyranny of this man and such the dread conceived of him in the minds of the natives, that no one durst complain or give information'.

Less is known of Umichand (also known variously as Omichand, Amin Chand or Amir Chand), who is not believed to have ever held any official position under the Calcutta Presidency but who nevertheless wielded great influence. He is said to have been a Sikh (some sources say Jain), businessman from

Amritsar who came to Calcutta in the early years of the Presidency, around 1715. After forty years of trading he had accumulated vast wealth and the influence which went with it. He financed many of the private trading enterprises which the clerks, or 'writers' of the East India Company were allowed to undertake and provided the finance for the construction of most of the mansions built by the British in 'White Town' adjacent to the old Fort William. He himself had a large house there as well as a grand garden villa located in the then north-eastern outskirts of Calcutta adjacent to the current day Nandanbagan. Contemporary accounts describe him as long bearded and enormously obese; his sumptuously clothed and bejewelled form requiring transport in a specially strengthened coach.

Umichand had a further important role, one that proved to be his later undoing. He acted as a special intermediary between the Presidency Council and the Nawab of Bengal, Siraj ud-Daula. Years of deteriorating relations between the British and the Nawab made Umichand's role as intermediary even more influential but increasingly unenviable, forced as he was to constantly juggle loyalties with an eye always to his own longer term self interest. When hostilities broke out in 1756 he appears to have taken his eye off the ball, being caught in possession of letters from the Nawab which clearly pointed to his treachery to the British. In consequence, he was imprisoned in Fort William, not being freed until the City fell to the Nawab's armies in June of that same year. Following the subsequent defeat of the Nawab at the Battle of Plassey and the re-establishment of the Presidency in Calcutta, Umichand, ever with an eye to the main chance, now sought to re-ingratiate himself with the British. He was, to some extent, successful in this, having assured Robert Clive of how pleased he was to see the Presidency back in control. He died shortly after in 1758 of a fever, according to some sources following a descent into insanity.

From Girish Park metro station, walk eastwards along Vivekananda Road right to the junction with Bidhan Sarani. The north western corner of this junction is occupied by the Swami Vivekananda ancestral home and cultural centre. Within the complex there is also an older building, locally called Chatterjee's House, which dates back to the 1820's. The building contains two Siva temples where it is said that the Swami's mother Bhubneswari Devi, was a regular worshiper.

Swami Vivekananda (1863-1902), a native of Calcutta, whose pre-monastic, birth name was Narendranath Dutta, was a greatly revered Hindu sage, spiritual leader and one of the most influential social reformers of 19th century India. He was one of the pre-eminent disciples of Ramakrishna and, uniquely at that time, travelled extensively on lecture tours accross America and Europe. He is widely credited with restoring pride amongst Hindus by heralding the ancient teachings of Hinduism onto the world religious stage. The enormous influence of Vivekananda and his teachings had great impact on nearly all of India's future leaders and amongst all those involved in the independence movement.

His earlier monastic years were spent wandering India as a penniless mendicant. On one such journey he reached the southernmost tip of mainland India at Kanyakumari in 1892. He is there reported to have swam the sea channel separating the town from a rock island where he meditated for three days on the past, present and future of India. Those who have travelled that far south will know of the famous Vivekananda temple now sited upon that rock island.

Turning into Bidhan Sarani, continue walking northwards for about 50 metres until, on your left, you find the entrance to Hari Pada Dutta Lane, identified with a fine old cast iron street nameplate. This tiny, narrow residential thoroughfare is typical of the many such lanes to be found throughout this part of north Calcutta. You could spend hours just navigating these charming lanes, the conservation value of which, hopefully is recognised by the Calcutta Municipal Corporation. Perhaps, one day an enterprising post-graduate architecture or town planning student from Calcutta University will secure funding to undertake a full survey and appraisal of these lanes and the buildings within them: I do hope so.

A little way along Hari Pada Dutta Lane, another, equally narrow lane, Madan Ghosh Lane, leads off to the right before performing a sharp left turn into Dr. N. Roy Sarani. Walk southwards and the first turning on you left returns you, via Hari Pada Dutta Lane, to Bidham Sarani.

When walking these and other lanes around north Calcutta pay particular attention to the mailboxes of the houses. Not only do they verify the name of the thoroughfare you are in but in most cases also tell you the profession or occupation of the head of the household; great fun for the particularly nosey, such as myself. One of my particular favourites is to be found eastwards in Brindaban Mullick Lane where the mailbox of a Mr Prasanta Banerjee proclaims him to be a Professor of Magic.

Back on Bidhan Sarani, a further 50 metres north brings you to the junction with Ramdulal Sarker Street on your left. On the opposite, tree lined side of Bidhan Sarani is the entrance to Hedua-Azad Hind Bagh, a large park complete with swimming pool. Just a little further north from this point and fronting the western side of Bidhan Sarani is the Bethune College and School, a reputed educational establishment for women, affiliated to the University of Calcutta. The College was founded in the 1840's by John Elliot Drinkwater Bethune who, amongst other posts held in the Calcutta Presidency Council, was President of the Council for Education. Following his early death in 1851, the then Governor General, Lord

Dalhousie took over responsibility for further development of the College. Located just to the rear of the main College buildings is a thoroughfare named Bethune Row, commemorating the College's founder.

From the junction of Bidhan Sarani and Ramdulal Sarker Street, walk westwards along the latter and once past the Girish Park Police Station, take the second turning on your right into Anath Babu's Bazar Lane. This opens out into an interesting, small but busy market dealing mainly in foodstuffs. The fruit and vegetable traders here seem to have a particular artistic flair judging by their superb displays. Much of this market is under cover, providing some welcome shade whilst you browse.

The Market leads out onto Dani Ghosh Sarani (as this part of Beadon Street is now known), very close to the busy Jatindra Mohan Avenue (the northern extension of Chitteranjan Avenue) crossing. Crossing to the western arm of Jatindra Mohan Avenue, 50 metres on, to your left, is the white fronted Minerva Theatre. Built in 1893, the Minerva was erected on the site of the Great National Theatre which had first opened in 1873. The Minerva played an important part in the Bengali cultural renaissance, having close association with Girish Chandra Ghose who gave the last great performance of his life here. The Theatre was badly damaged by fire in 1922 but was restored three years later. Further extensive refurbishment of the Theatre was completed in 2007.

Walking westwards past the Theatre, you quickly reach the junction with Rabindra Sarani. At this south eastern corner of the junction is Rabindra Kanan, a decent sized park and open space, popular with students. This area once formed the grounds of the main residence of Raja Nuncomar (also spelled Nando Kumar); who, with Warren Hastings and Sir Elijah Impey, formed the principal dramatis personae of a particularly controversial episode of the 18th century Calcutta Presidency. The 'Nuncomar Incident'[6] culminated in the execution of Nuncomar and contributed to the later impeachment of both Hastings and Impey.

Leaving Rabindra Kanan and crossing to the western side of Rabindra Sarani, the first turning to your right is Tagore Castle Street. This busy narrow Street leads into the broader, and even busier, Tagore Castle Road. A hectic food market occupies the eastern end of this Road along with a small colony of scavangers' shanties: the large piles of, as yet unsorted, rubbish heaped about providing the clue to the trade followed by the occupants.

As you walk westwards along the Road your attention is drawn to a structure which appears peculiarly out of place in these surroundings. Here is what, at first glimpse, looks very much like a castle complete with turrets and battlements. This is precisely what it is, Tagore Castle, built in the mid 19th century by Jantindra Mohan Tagore, and clearly influenced by his travels in Europe, particularly in Scotland. The mix of architectural styles which has gone into this building is little short of fantastic. Apart from the turrets and battlements, the weather vanes and the clock tower, there are stepped gables, oriel and arrow slit windows and balconies of several designs, all married together with classic Rajasthan flourishes. This is the rear view of the building; the frontage is best viewed from Prasanna Kumar (P.K. for short) Tagore Street which runs parallel. To get there, simply take the next turning on the left then left again. Tagore Castle, which is listed by Calcutta Municipal Corporation as a heritage building, is in a truly deplorable state of repair and is probably only kept standing by the numerous, hideous and no doubt illegal concrete extensions that have been tacked onto the original structure with random

---

[6]See Annexe 1 - Historical Notes

abandonment. Today, it appears to be in use as a sprawling tenement building, chock-a-block with tenants whose ragged laundry hangs from the once graceful balconies.

There are other surprising buildings in P.K. Tagore Street. Just west of the Tagore Castle and set back from the road, is an enormous old mansion, reminiscent of the Old Mint building, with a fine, colonnaded frontage and a parade of roofline statuary. Sadly, this appears to be in a bad state of repair. At number 10 is the old Metropolitan Institute, built in the last quarter of the 19th century and still providing useful service, now as a post office. All along this part of P.K Tagore Street most of what could be used as a footpath is taken over by the commerce of small traders in vegetables, fresh fish and handy household items. I once bought an excellent and brightly coloured nylon scrubbing brush here; no doubt being roundly swindled in the process.

Walking eastwards to the end of P.K. Tagore Street, cross Rabindra Sarani and opposite you will find the entrance to Set Bagan Gullee. This narrow passage is immediately recognisable by the groups of garishly clad working ladies who generally congregate here. At the end of the Gullee turn left and, walking northwards, in a few minutes you will emerge into Ramesh Dutta Street. There will be no mistaking your arrival there since the Street is a centre for a kind of heavy metal bashing industry which is conducted all over the thoroughfare and from numerous small workshops here and in the adjoining by-lanes. The air is filled with fearful noises of scores of heavy hammers striking on iron plate; the Banshee howl of angle grinders showering passers-by in fountains of golden sparks; and the acrid odours from oxy-acetylene torches slicing hotly through steel, mixed up with those blinding blue-white flashes and distinct popping noises of electric arc welders.

All this symphony of industry is hard on the hearing even out in the open air; within the workshops it is deafening. The air temperature is hovering around 37 degrees C. in the shade (except that out in the Street there is little shade to be had). Within the workshops, constructed mainly of corrugated tin, and additionally heated by glowing furnaces of coals, it is so stifling that it becomes difficult to breathe. Here men, youths and quite young boys work for hours on end; it is like a scene out of Dante's Inferno.

All this industry is conducted in a manner that would cause apoplexy in any health and safety zealot from the west. I have never, ever seen a welding mask or goggles being used, yet alone any form of protective clothing, even gloves. Most of the workers are either barefoot or shod only in rubber flip-flops even when handling heavy iron plate.

The product of all this labour is stacked outside the workshops and all along the Street. Some of it is easily identifiable, enormous iron cooking pots, wrought iron window grills, steel shop shutters, fabricated steel beams and the like. Other items, their use can only be guessed at. There are enormous cauldron shaped iron receptacles in which you could boil all three of Macbeth's witches at the same time and still have plenty of room to spare. Strange, large square and rectangular tank like vessels complete with opening hatches and welded on access ladders looking rather like beached landing craft.

Ramesh Dutta Street together with the adjoining lanes radiating east and south, form the area known as Rambagan. Regarded by many Calcuttans as an insalubrious slum, Rambagan is not wholly unloved; I am one of those who happen to like the place for its vibrancy, friendly and industrious people and its facility to continually surprise. It is the sort of place (and there are many such others in Calcutta), where you can meet with the unexpected around every twist or corner and frequently do.

It was in Rambagan that I first encountered the hand- made paper bag industry. Buy anything loose from a small trader in a Calcutta street and you are likely to be handed your purchase in a bag, intricately fashioned from recycled sheets of newspaper. These bags come in all shapes and sizes and are minor works of art. They form one of the staple cottage industries of the bustees in places like Rambagan. All that is needed is old, cleanish newspapers, a pot of paste and considerable dexterity to perform the origami required. Small, nimble hands are ideally suited to the task and in consequence, many children are employed in this trade. It is not as easy as it is made to appear; I know, I have tried it and made a complete mess of the job, much to the amusement of my temporary tutor, Sanjit. Sanjit is about 13 years of age, the eldest of his family's four children. He lives in a nearby bustee and says he has been doing this work for the last 4 years. He will make up to 500 bags per shift, for which he receives 40 to 50 Rupees depending on the sizes he is producing. The young artisans like Sanjit are not of course in this line of business on their own account, but are supplied with materials and paid on a piecework basis by the middleman (who is an almost omnipresent institution in Indian commerce), who then sells on the product to the suppliers.

The eastern end of Ramesh Dutta Street performs a sharp right turn into Dayal Mitra Lane which, once across Jogen Dutta Lane, becomes Azul Mullick Lane. This Lane leads out of Rambagan and into Jatindra Mohan Avenue at a point about half way between the Beadon Street and Vivekananda Road crossings. Walking southwards for about 100 metres returns you to your starting point, the Girish Park metro station.

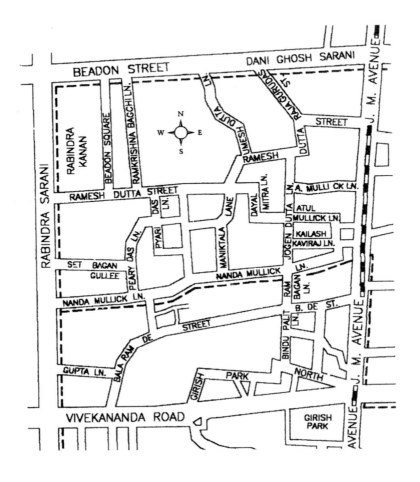

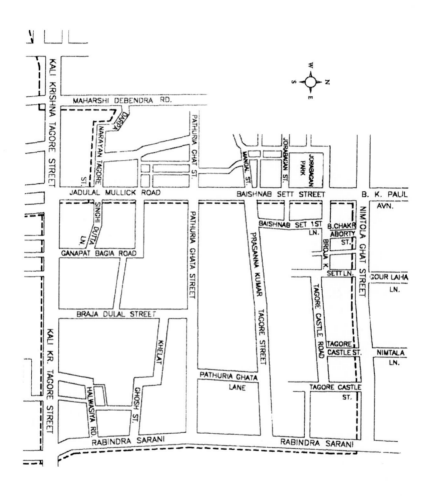

CHAPTER 8

Amherst Street (North & Central) and Burtolla (South)

This walk takes in those parts of the Amherst Street and Burtolla areas which lay between Beadon Street in the north and Keshab Sen Street to the south. Bidhan Sarani forms the western boundary and the Circular Canal the eastern boundary. The nearest metro stations serving these areas are Girish Park to the north and M.G. Road to the south although both are a good 10 to 15 minute walk west of Bidhan Sarani.

A good starting point is the junction of Beadon Street and Bidhan Sarani. To get there, turn left out of Girish Park metro station and walk northwards along Jatindra Mohan Avenue until you reach the Beadon Street crossing. Turn right here and continue east along Beadon Street for about 200 metres until you reach the junction with Bidhan Sarani.

East of Bidhan Sarani, Beadon Street becomes Abhedananda Road. The large park and swimming pool, Hedua-Azad Hind Bagh, occupies the south eastern corner of the junction and stretches southwards for about 100 metres, providing a pleasant, tree shaded setting.

Just behind the Park is the Scottish Church College, accessed via Urquhart Square which is the first turning on the right off Abhedananda Road. This renowned co-educational institution was founded by the Rev. Dr. Alexander Duff, of whom mention has been made earlier in this work. Originally established in 1830 as the General Assembly's Institution, the College is the oldest currently operating, missionary administered educational establishment in India. It is housed in a very fine Palladian building dating back to 1839, behind handsome iron gates set between classical twin lodges. Notable past alumni of the College include Swami Vivekananda and Subhas Chandra Bose.

Just past the College campus, Urquhart Square meets Sisir Bhaduri Sarani. Turn left here and then left again into Duff Street. This thoroughfare, which links Vivekananda Road to the south with Bidhan Sarani to the north, contains some interesting 19th century residential buildings and a number of schools. At the northern end of the Street, just before it joins Bidhan Sarani, a turning to the right leads into Duff Lane which performs a kind of horseshoe with offshoots both to the south and to the east. This quiet and unspoilt residential backwater epitomises the timeless charm of north Calcutta and is of high conservation value, even down to the many cast iron, white on blue, street nameplates found hereabouts.

This is just the sort of place to bump into a Ful Jharu Wallah and was exactly what I did when turning a blind corner whilst once exploring a narrow lane in this neighbourhood. Where the line of sight is less obstructed, the Ful Jharu Wallah is an easy chap to spot from a distance on account that he will be carrying, sloped to his shoulder, a bundle of long poles, each adorned at the upper end with a kind of vivedly coloured feather duster. These cleaning sticks (ful jharu), which can measure 2 to 3 metres in length, are his stock in trade which he will hawk around Calcutta's residential districts. The Ful Jharu Wallah's wares are clearly meant to be employed in dusting those hard to reach corners although just why they need to be quite so long for ordinary dwellings, I have never discovered;

perhaps it is traditional. The day cannot be far away when some Bengali entrepreneur will corner the market by introducing the telescopic ful jharu. But somehow, 'telescopic Ful Jharu Wallah' does not have quite the same ring to it.

The eastern spur of Duff Lane connects with the short and narrow Hari Pal 2nd Lane. Turning left into this Lane brings you back out onto Bidhan Sarani. Just east of this point is the Ananda Ashram at number 21/2. It is said that in this building, in the early 19th century, the inaugural meeting of the Brahmo Samaj movement was held. This religious movement, founded in Calcutta in 1828 by the social reformer Raja Ram Mohan Roy, now has branches worldwide. The movement propounds that there is but one God who is omnipresent and omniscient and does not believe in idolatry or the caste system. One of the movement's most famous luminaries was Rabindranath Tagore.

The next turning on your right off Bidhan Sarani is the northern end of Hartaki Bagan Lane, almost a twin of Hari Pal 2nd Lane. At the southern end of this Lane, turn left into the main Hari Pal Lane and walk eastward until the Lane joins Raja Gopi Mohan Street. You will notice that, on reaching this point, the streets are far busier than those you have just left behind. The level of activity increases as you cross Raja Gopi Mohan Street and walk southwards. The reason for the increasing bustle is explained as you take the first turning to your left into the start of Manicktala Bazar Lane. The trading and movement of goods all along this Lane is but nothing compared to the activity going on in the Bazar itself. This is to be found at the eastern extremity of the Lane where it joins Acharya Prafulla Chandra (A.P.C.) Road and easily identified by its landmark, domed clock tower. The Maniktala Bazar, said to be one of the oldest in Calcutta, occupies the whole north western corner of the very busy A.P.C. Road crossing, more generally known locally as the 'Manicktala Crossing'.

Manicktala, the name by which this area is known, is derived from 'Manik Pir', the name of a mosque in the vicinity.

The Bazar itself, which is mainly under cover, comprises a maze of narrow walkways between the stalls of literally hundreds of traders. Following the usual layout, general goods and clothing are to be found mainly around the perimeter of the Bazar, with the more central areas being given over to foodstuffs. You can find here a wide variety of fruit and vegetables, rice, pulses, herbs and spices. There is a large section where a brisk trade in fresh fish is conducted and where the walkways can get very slippery underfoot. You can find this and the meat section easily by simply following your nose.

Sadly, it seems that this ancient Bazar's days may be numbered as there are proposals for demolition and redevelopment of the site at some, as yet undetermined date. If this happens, it will be a great loss to north Calcutta.

Leaving the Bazar via the eastern exit onto A.P.C. Road, the large building facing you on the north eastern corner of the Manicktala Crossing, is the Central Blood Bank for West Bengal. Turning south down A.P.C. Road and once across Vivekananda Road, looking back you get the best view of the Bazar's splendid domed clock tower. On you right is the popular Chaya Cinema, rumoured to screen the raciest X rated Hindi films in all of Calcutta. Just past the Cinema is the Manicktala Wine Shop where, through the inevitable heavy iron grill, you can negotiate the purchase of bottles of imported or indigenous liquor.

One hundred metres or so further south but on the other side of A.P.C. Road is a large white six storey, building housing the Leprosy Mission's Premananda Memorial Hospital. Of the approximate 300,000 new cases of Leprosy diagnosed world-wide each year, just fewer than 70% occur in India. Leprosy has been well described as 'a disease apart' because of the physical impairments, stigma and poverty associated with it. Still surrounded by myths and fear of ostracism, it remains more than just a medical condition and one which can make sufferers reluctant to disclose their symptoms at an early enough stage to facilitate a complete cure. Just behind the Hospital is an old Christian cemetery, now in a deplorable condition.

Almost opposite the Hospital, on the western side of A.P.C. Road at number 113, is a neat gated compound containing a collection of handsome buildings set in beautiful grounds. This is the office of Calcutta's Deputy Commissioner of Police and also houses the marvellous Calcutta Police Museum. A visit here is a must for any traveller interested in the history of the City. The grandeur of these buildings is explained by the fact that from 1814 to 1830, they formed the principal residence of Raja Ram Mohan Roy. You will need to report to the guard post just inside the compound gates before walking straight on to the Museum building which is set back further in the grounds. The Museum is open every day except Mondays and public holidays, between the hours of 11.00 am and 5.00 pm. No advance booking is required.

Housed on two floors, the well thought out and presented displays trace the organisation and development of the Calcutta Police from the earliest days of the 18th century until the present day. The displays include notes on celebrated cases together with related exhibits from the police investigations. Many such cases relate to the freedom struggle against British rule and have considerable historical significance. To those travellers who have journeyed as far east as Port Blair in India's Andaman Islands and visited the Cellular Jail there, some of the names of those involved in these cases will strike a familiar chord. Many of those convicted freedom fighters served their sentences in that far flung island prison which has now been declared a National Monument.

Amongst the displays are included copies of numerous direc-
tives issued by long dead Commissioners of Police which give a
sideways view of the development of social norms in Calcutta
down the centuries. Amongst my favourites are those urging
officers to take tougher action against such anti-social activities
as 'kite flying' and 'furious driving' (of carriages) in the Bow
Bazar area. On the staircase to the upper floor displays, stands
the casing of a World War II, Japanese bomb dropped on Hatibagan Bazar but which, thankfully, failed to explode.

The Museum staff who are welcoming, well informed and very
helpful, will invite you to write your comments in the
Museum's vistors' book.

On leaving the Museum compound, continue south along A.P.C.
Road taking the next turning on the right into Mahendra Srimani
Street. Fifty metres on, to your left, is a by-lane which leads into
a sort of grid pattern of inter-connecting small lanes. The first
such lane is Ramakrishna Das Lane from which a further three
small by-lanes lead south into Badur Bagan Lane. There are some
interesting old residential buildings along these lanes, some with
particularly pleasing ironwork balconies and arcading.

It was whilst exploring these Lanes that I once encountered a
cloud of dust billowing from the open doorway of a house,
followed by an industrious householder emerging backwards
into the street, bent low and furiously sweeping with one of
those brooms comprising a bundle of long twigs bound
together at one end. So absorbed was he in his endeavours that
he backed straight into me, covering my sandals in miscellaneous debris and dust. A smiled apology and that very Indian
sideways nodding of the head and he was back to his labours
with renewed vigour and I was on my way.

Badur Bagan Lane leads west where is joins Brindaban Mullick
Lane, running north to south. This thoroughfare contains some

superb buildings many of which, because of their impressive frontages, were clearly built at a time when they could be viewed from further back than the current lay-out of the adjoining buildings allows. The majority of these buildings appear still to be primarily residential. There is one in particular, a large white four storey structure which sports heraldic beasts set along the pediment. There is a lion rampant and a unicorn and what looks very much like a coat of arms. Unfortunately the Lane is too narrow to allow a better, less acute angle of view. Behind the western side of the Lane is Hrishikesh Park which fronts Amherst Street, accessed by either of the two by-lanes running along each side of the Park. The Park contains a pumping station, one of a series designed to prevent flooding in the area from heavy monsoon rains. Boats used to be quite a common sight at such times along Amherst Street. According to some, the presence of boats is still quite common, particularly when the drainage outfall, located near the Circular Road, silts up bringing the pumping station's efforts to nought.

Heading south along Amherst Street you soon come to the area's Police Station. Almost opposite the Police Station and leading off the western side of the Street just past the City College campus, is Bechu Chatterjee Street. Take the second turning on your left off Bechu Chatterjee Street into Jhamapukur Lane and walk southwards to the junction of Keshab Sen Street. Just by this junction is a business trading in nothing but sheet rubber, piles of it heaped all over the footpath, everything from rubber door mats to carpet like rolls of the stuff, some smooth, some ribbed, all in various thicknesses; a fetishist's paradise.

Turning right and walking westwards along Keshab Sen Street you soon reach the junction with Bidhan Sarani. Just north of this junction and fronting onto Bidhan Sarani, is the Yhudi Market; worth a look particularly since, being largely under cover, it provides some welcome shade. On the pavement outside the Market you will find a kind of mini enterprise seen all over Calcutta; the 'Wojon Wallah', the man with a pair of bathroom scales which you can use to weigh yourself. His fee, for the use of his equipment, is rarely more than one rupee and often the service includes him writing your weight on a slip of paper and handing it to you. I make it a point always to use the services of these enterprising chaps, if only to see how accurate their scales are. I have found that I have often lost or gained 5 or 6 kilos in the space of less than half a kilometre.

Continuing northwards along Bidhan Sarani you pass the famous temple Thanthania Kalibari to your right just before the junction with the eastern end of Muktaram Babu Street. A little further on, also on your right is the Srimani Market, a lively bustling place selling mainly foodstuffs. Almost opposite the Market on the eastern side of Bidhan Sarani is the premises of Ghose and Co., a noted sweet shop of north Calcutta, popular with those with a sweet tooth. Just past the Srimani Market you reach the major junction with Vivekananda Road. Turning left here and walking westwards for about 150 metres brings you to the Chitteranjan Avenue crossing and the Girish Park metro station.

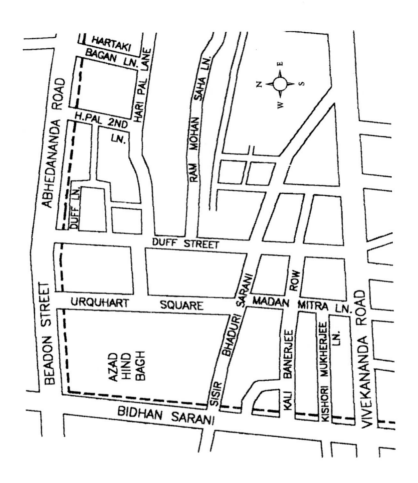

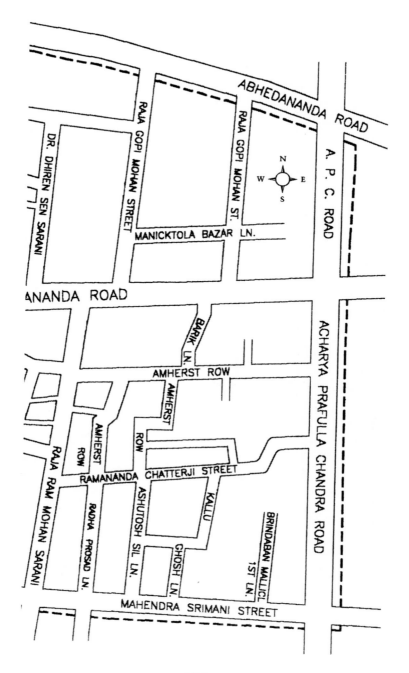

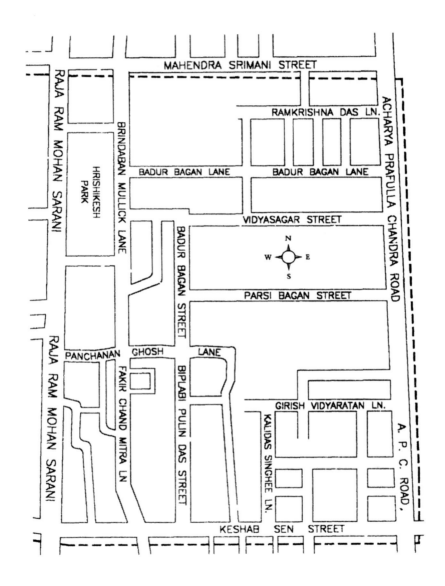

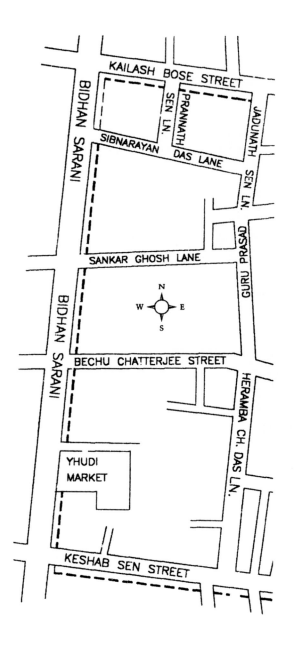

CHAPTER 9

Burtolla (North)
and Jorabagan (North)

This walk takes in the that part of the Jorabagan area sand-wiched between B.K. Pal Avenue to the north, Nimtala Ghat Street to the south and Rabindra Sarani and the River Hooghly to the east and west respectively. Also covered is the larger part of the Burtolla area between Sri Arabinda Sarani to the north, Beadon Street to the south and east of Rabindra Sarani as far as Bidhan Sarani. This area is served by Girish Park and Sovabazar metro stations, the former being located almost equidistant between the eastern and western bound-aries of the combined areas and the latter located centrally along the northern boundary.

A good starting point is the Sovabazar metro station at the junction of Jantrindra Mohan Avenue (the northern externsion of Chitteranjan Avenue) and Sri Arabinda Sarani. The Burtolla area, which forms the first part of this walk is split centrally by Jatindra Mohan Avenue and the areas to the east and west of this dividing line could not be more different. The eastern section is primarily residential and relatively quiet in character. The western section includes Sonagachi, Calcutta's most infa-mous red light district.

Walking east along Sri Arabinda Sarani (formerly Grey Street), to the junction with Bidhan Sarani, the area immediately to the north of this point is known as Hatibagan and this junction the Hatibagan Crossing. The Hatibagan Bazar is to be found on the northern side of the Crossing. It was around Hatibagan Crossing that the diminutive sixty year old, Lakshmi Das spent almost forty years begging for alms. Named after the Hindu goddess of wealth, Lakshmi would set aside a small part of her daily earnings to provide living expenses for when she retired. She kept these saved coins in buckets at the shanty in which she lived alone in Nandanbagan and after retirement, drew on these funds for her daily needs. Following an attempted theft of her nest egg, neighbours alerted the Police who removed four full buckets of coins weighing nearly 100 kilos in total, for safekeeping at nearby Burtolla Police Station. The Police contacted the manager of the local branch of the Central Bank of India, who agreed to open a savings account for Lakshmi. It took bank staff several days to count the mass of coins which ranged from the old one paise coin to the new five rupee coin. In total Lakshmi's accumulated savings amounted to 20,788 rupees (just over £260) at current exchange rates: a sobering lesson in frugality. May Lakshmi's retirement be long and happy.

Just south of the Hatibagan Crossing, on the eastern side of Bidhan Sarani, stands the famous New Star Theatre. This grand and highly ornate building was completed in 1888 and extensively restored and refurbished as recently as 2006. This historic venue, now a cultural centre, theatre and cinema, boasts a fine auditorium of 500 plus seats.

Just south of the Theatre, off the western side of Bidhan Sarani, is Hemendra Sen Street. This leads through to Hari Ghose Street, a significant thoroughfare running north to south and parallel to Bidhan Sarani. Opposite Hemendra Sen Street is the eastern end of Masjid Bari Street. This ancient Street leads by a series of twists and turns all the way westward to Rabindra Sarani, indicating that it was once a single unbroken thoroughfare until divided by the laying out of Jatindra Mohan Avenue. The Street performs a graceful curve to the left then a ninety degree turn to the right. At this point and opposite is Jaggernath Suri Lane, which, leading south, connects Masjid Bari Street with Durga Charan Mitra Street. Like the former, this Street also runs westwards, crossing Jatindra Mohan Avenue, and on all the way to Rabindra Sarani. This eastern stretch is primarily residential with some interesting examples of domestic architecture, particularly in the many lanes running north and south off the Street. This is just the sort of place where you are likely to find a Shaan Wallah; the itinerant knife grinder who tours neighbourhoods such as this in search of clients. He carries strung to his back, a contraption which looks a little like a fold-up unicycle. Once he secures a commission, his apparatus is unfolded and set up. The cycle wheel drives his grinding stone as he sits showering sparks into the street from whatever it is he is sharpening. Curiously, at one time knife grinders used to be a fairly familiar sight in the streets of British cities but are rarely if ever seen now.

Where Durga Charan Mitra Street meets Jatindra Mohan Avenue, turn left and walk southwards for about 150 metres until you are almost at the Beadon Street Crossing. To your left is a large house built in the 1930's by a noted ophthalmologist, Dr Kamala Hazari. Once known as 'Tiger House' on account of the brace of Royal Bengal Tigers the Doctor kept there as pets, the building is also unusual in that it was one of the first to include a cellar (unusual given the tricky sub-soil conditions of Calcutta), and had fitted an early form of wind turbine with which to generate electricity.

Crossing Jatindra Mohan Avenue at this point, turn right into Beadon Street, keeping to the northern pavement. Most Calcuttans refer to the general area to the north of here, sandwiched between Jatindra Mohan Avenue and Rabindra Sarani as Sonagachi although the red light district proper does not really begin until a street or two further north. There has been more coverage given to the small area that is Sonagachi than to the whole of the rest of North Calcutta put together. Whilst some of this has been informed and useful comment, rather more has ranged from inaccurate hearsay through to the nonsensical.

Sonagachi, which means 'Golden Tree', has had long association with the world's oldest profession. In the 18th and 19th centuries it was the place where many a merchant housed his mistresses. Today it is a place where thousands of sex workers (which is the term they prefer to prostitute), sell their bodies from brothels housed in decaying buildings ranged along the narrow, thronged thoroughfares which make up the area. Some put the number of sex-workers operating in Sonagachi as high as ten thousand; other sources quote a more probable figure of around six thousand. As with Calcutta's other red light districts, this is by no means all that goes on here; there is also taking place a good deal of the more mundane and routine day to day activities of families living in and around the area. Again in common with these other red light districts, here there is visible evidence of a level of co-existence of different lifestyles which it is difficult to imagine being replicated so successfully in corresponding districts of western cities. This may be due, in part at least, to the fact that, in India prostitution is driven mainly by simple poverty rather than the high levels of drug-dependency so much more in evidence in the west.

Rupali Das is a 34 year old sex-worker who works in Sonagachi and resides in the nearby Rambagan bustee. She was originally from the Hugli area, about 40 kilometres upriver from Calcutta, where she had been a housewife and mother to her two infant children. After being deserted by her husband when she was 23, she came to Calcutta in search of a livelihood. She was sold to a Mahajan (a money lender in the sex trade), and has been a sex-worker ever since. Her earnings are around 300 to 400 Rupees a day (£3.75 to £5.10) of which half has to be paid over to the madam of the premises from which she works. Her monthly income, after these 'deductions' is therefore just under 5,000 Rupees (about £62). From this she pays 1,100 Rupees in rent, 300 Rupees for electricity, 1,200 to 1,400 for food and fuel and 500 Rupees in private tuition fees for her children, a total average monthly outgoing of about 3,200 Rupees (£41). Some of the balance has to provide for clothing and other incidental expenses but what is left is saved against the day when her earnings start to decrease with advancing age. She considers herself fortunate in the financial sense but, as the family's breadwinner, worries about illness which could prevent her from working.

Provided the western traveller adopts a common sense approach and an etiquette grounded in basic good manners, navigating Sonagachi during the daytime need present no difficulties. Be aware of where you are, look as if you know your way about and appreciate just how much you stick out. Do not attempt, uninvited, to photograph any of the ladies; it is after all their place of work and any interest shown in them, unless on a professional level, is unlikely to be appreciated. After dark, Sonagachi takes on a rather different and less predictable character. It is then that the area experiences its biggest influx of potential clients, some of whom will have been drinking, often heavily. At these times the traveller should steer clear of the place.

Walking westwards along Beadon Street, the third turning to your right is Garan Hatta Street. This Street performs a half crescent curve to the left before emerging onto Rabindra Sarani opposite the Oriental Seminary. This heritage building, houses the famous educational establishment which was founded in 1829 by Gour Mohan Addy. The Seminary, which moved to the present building in 1914, was the earliest private school for Hindu children in Calcutta. Before the founding of the Seminary, Indian pupils wishing to study English had to attend the missionary schools where they were subjected to Christian religious influence. The Seminary filled the gap by providing a school for learning English free of alien religious influences. Originally the Seminary was open to Hindu boys only but became co-educational in 1934. Rabindranath Tagore attended the Seminary as his first school but reportedly stayed only a brief time.

Turning right into Rabindra Sarani, less than 100 metres north is the western end of Durga Charan Mitra Street, the main thoroughfare of Sonagachi. On entering the Street, immediately to your left and set back a little, is the Allen Market, a small but very busy foodstuffs market. Running along the eastern boundary of the Market is Sonagachi Lane, the only geographical reference to Sonagachi to be found on any map of the City. This ancient and narrow lane contains some truly appalling habitations and is usually thronged with working ladies and sinister looking young men. It sounds intimidating but, actually is not, just a little different.

Although seemingly a blind alley, Sonagachi Lane does actually connect to Masjid Bari Street which runs roughly parallel to Durga Charan Mitra Street. Walking eastwards along Durga Charan Mitra Street the first turning on your left is Manruddin Lane. This is almost a replica of Sonagachi Lane but will be entered by the traveller with more trepidation as a sharp twist, midway along, obstructs sight of the other end which too emerges onto Masjid Bari Street. The narrowness of the lanes of Sonagachi is often accentuated by the height of the buildings lining either side. Whilst few of these exceed three stories, their measured height would be equal to three or four times the width of the thoroughfares in which they stand. This creates the impression of walking along a series of narrow, twisting and pullulating urban crevasses.

The next lane to the left is Imam Bux Lane which is altogether wider along the whole of its serpentine length until it emerges into Masjid Bari Street. Ramjoy Seal Lane is the next on the left. This is a blind alley, very narrow and equally uninviting. Opposite this blind alley is the northern end of Ram Chand Ghose Lane which leads back onto Beadon Street. Just east of the start of this Lane is a series of small, by-lanes usually thronged with sex-workers, both on and off duty (those on duty recognisable by being made up to the nines). These by-lanes form a kind of small square just where Durga Charan Mitra Street crosses Abinash Kaviraj Street. Here is the modest administrative office of the impressive 'Sonagachi Project'

The Sonagachi Project grew out of a study undertaken in 1992 by the All India Institute of Hygiene and Public Health into the prevalence of sexually transmitted illnesses and HIV infection amongst the sex-workers of Sonagachi. The Project, founded by Dr. Smarajit Jana, a public health scientist, set up a clinic in Sonagachi to treat syphilis and gonorrhoea and spread awareness of HIV and its prevention. From this base, the Project developed over the years into a full blown trade as-sociation or co-operative run by the sex-workers themselves. The Project employs scores of sex-workers to go from brothel to brothel spreading the gospel of the importance of using condoms as an effective shield against HIV infection and other sexually transmitted illnesses. Meeting resistance at first, the Project has organised a majority of the sex-workers in Sonagachi into a force with the influence to challenge any re-calcitrant pimp or madam objecting to the enforced use of condoms by clients. So strong has the influence of these com-bined sex-workers grown, that they are not adverse to picket-ing police stations demanding action against criminals operat-ing on their patch. They have also done much to combat child prostitution by rescuing, or reporting young girls sold or duped into the trade, although the desired removal of the strong competition these under-age girls pose, could also said to be a factor.

The 'Durbar' (Durbar Mahila Samanwaya Committee) as the co-operative is now known, makes some impressive claims for its work. It is claimed that condom use has risen from under 5% in 1992 to 90% today whilst HIV infection is estimated to be pegged around 5%, making it the lowest rate for any red light district of any Indian city. Even if the exact figures are disputed and they frequently are, there can be little doubt of the very considerable achievements of the 'Durbar'. Quite apart from the health benefits achieved, the 'Durbar' has organised very successful literacy classes where the literate sex-workers teach the illiterate. The organisation has also created a kind of credit union, freeing impoverished sex-workers from the clutches of avaricious money lenders, previously their only source of loans.

Where Durga Charan Mitra Street crosses Abinash Kaviraj Street turn left into the latter and, 50 metres on take the next turning on your left into Masjid Bari Street. This is Sonagachi's second main thoroughfare and is bustling with life. Small traders, paan sellers and chai stalls are dotted about everywhere, each attracting their own small clusters of clientele and general lookers on. Numerous tiny workshops open onto the Street, small hives of industry from which emerge the rattle of sewing machines, mixed smells of rubber, cellulose thinners and paint and the tap tap of small hammers crafting something intricate. Some of the buildings along the Street are ancient and crumbling; steep, narrow staircases just visible through open doorways. A few of these doorways boast a sort of mini temple decoration set into the stonework above the lintels; a feature unseen anywhere else in these walks around Calcutta.

Masjid Bari Street becomes less respectable looking the further west you walk. By the time you reach the junction with the northern end of Manruddin Lane, where the Street twists sharply to the left, there are unmistakable reminders of the ancient trade for which Sonagachi is best known. Where the

Street straightens out again, you pass the northern end of Sonagachi Lane and the Allen Market before emerging onto Rabindra Sarani.

Turn right into Rabindra Sarani then, taking the first turning on your right, enter Joy Mitra Street. The first thing you notice is the archaic spelling 'Mitter' for Mitra on the old cast iron street nameplate. This street provides a delightful walk, twisting and turning this way and that with many, unnamed gullees leading off to either side. There are numerous interesting residential buildings of considerable age along the whole length of this thoroughfare, interspersed with small shop premises, many of which use the 'Joy Mitter Street' spelling incorporated into their name boards. There are usually a few games of street cricket going on hereabouts; juvenile bowlers and batsmen who may one day appear for India. It was here that I was once importuned by a dozen or more clamouring youngsters, anxious that I rule on whether a catch where the ball had first bounced off a wall was allowed. I had not a clue but confidently brazened it out by suggesting that if the ball had not actually touched the ground first, then it was a good catch. The astonishing thing was that they all seemed to accept this, thanking me profusely for my sound judgement. I moved on guiltily, having possibly reinforced the myth that all Englishmen are experts on the game.

The Street eventually meets Abinash Kaviraj Street where, if you turn left and walk 50 metres north, brings you out into the major thoroughfare of Sri Arabinda Sarani. Turning left here and walking westwards quickly brings you to the next major junction, which is the Butto Kristo Pal Avenue crossing. The long graceful curve of the Avenue cuts accross Rabindra Sarani and continues westwards, passing the small but pleasantly shaded B.K. Pal Park on the right, until you reach number 40 where, abruptly it turns southwards. Opposite, at this point and located next door to a Kali Temple, is a busy Community

Hall, often thronged with the guests to the many wedding parties held there.

Less than 100 metres further south, the Avenue meets Nimtala Ghat Street. Just to your right, at number 76, is Jorabagan police station, housed in a magnificent old mansion set amidst a canopy of trees. This officially listed heritage building once housed the General Assembly Institution and Free Church of Scotland founded by the Rev. Alexander Duff.

Walking westwards along Nimtala Ghat Street towards the Hooghly you will notice the many timber merchants operating here. Curiously, their stocks appear to be almost exclusively of lengths not exceeding about one metre. These are the suppliers of the fuel used for the traditional cremation pyres at the burning ghats which are located a little further to the west.

As you draw near to an ancient Mosque, found to your right, the Street performs a kind of chicane before meeting Strand Bank Road and the River. The burning ghats are located along here, fronting the River about 50 metres north of this point and opposite a large Kali Temple. The cremation ground is respectfully shielded both from the roadside and from the river. Within the complex is located the Bootnath Temple for devotees of Shiva. Nowadays, most of the 90 or so cremations which take place here daily are dealt with by the electric furnaces recently installed by the Calcutta Municipal Corporation although a tenth of this number are still cremated on the traditional wooden pyres. The people who handle the bodies to be cremated here (and indeed corpses in hospitals or morgues generally) are called Doms and are considered an untouchable caste.

The Nimtala Burning Ghat is now an officially listed heritage building.

For those wishing to return by a different route, the Ahritola Ghat can be found 100 metres further north. Passenger ferries call here en route downriver to the Howrah Ghat, just south of the Howrah Bridge and upriver to Sovabazar and Bagbazar Ghats. To return to your starting point via the ferry, get out at Sovabazar Ghat and directly opposite the ferry ramp is Sovabazar Street which, walking eastwards, leads you back to the Sovabazar metro station.

An alternative is to retrace your steps back along Nimtala Ghat Street to the Jorabagan Police Station, then continue eastwards along the Street to the junction with Rabindra Sarani. Just before this junction, you pass, on your left, the massive crumbling edifice of what was originally Duff College, subsequently Rajabagan Thana and thereafter abandoned to squatters. This once magnificent building is in a deplorable condition and is now in all likelihood beyond saving. It is said that not even squatters will now enter the building, so dangerous has the structure become. Crossing Rabindra Sarani into Beadon Street, directly opposite, continue eastwards past the Minerva Theatre on your right until you meet Jatindra Mohan Avenue. Turning south here, Girish Park metro station can be found about 200 metres further on.

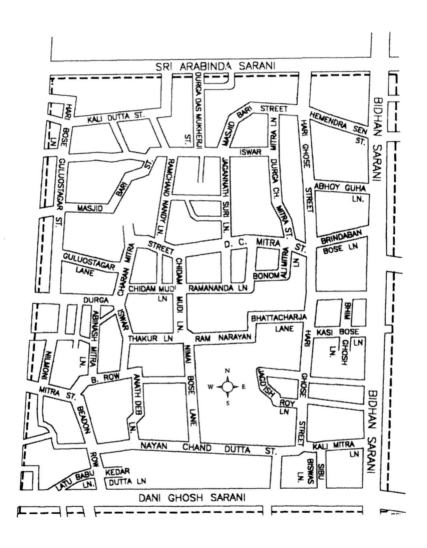

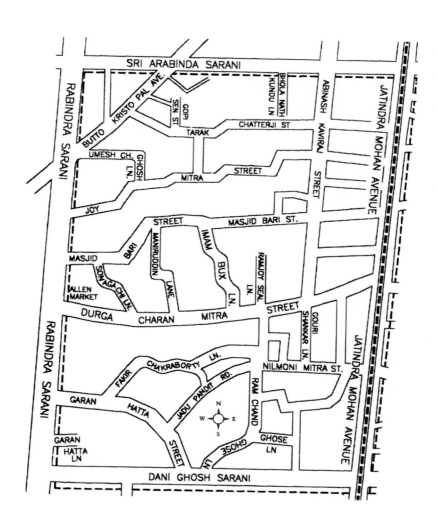

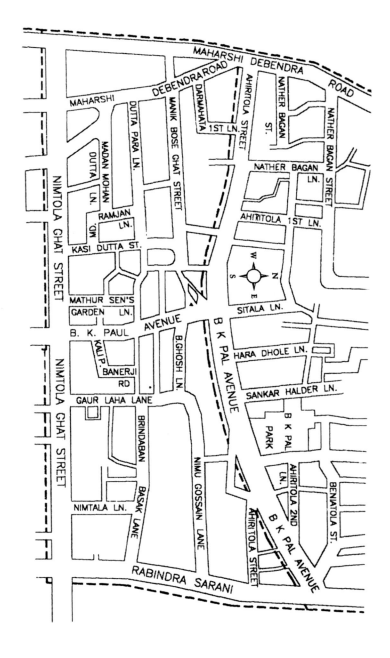

CHAPTER 10

Taltala and Muchipara (South)

This walk takes in the most south easterly of all the areas covered in this work and includes the greater part of Taltala and the southern parts of Muchipara. These combined areas are enclosed by Muzzaffar Ahmed Street to the south, B.B. Ganguly Street to the north and Mirza Ghalib Street and Acharya Jagadish Chandra Bose (A.J.C. Bose) Road to the west and east respectively. The areas are served by Park Street, Esplanade and Chandni Chowk metro stations, all of which lay along the western extremities.

A convenient starting point is the junction of Park Street and Mirza Ghalib Street (erstwhile Free School Street). To get there from Park Street metro station, walk eastwards along Park Street, past the Asiatic Society building and the Park Hotel and Mirza Ghalib Street is then the first turning on your left. From here walk northwards along the Street and take the third turning on your right into Colin Lane. The general area east of this point is Taltala, one of the older quarters of Calcutta and predominantly Muslim. Taltala is a place criss-crossed with pullulating lanes and busy bazaars. It is one of the few places left in Calcutta where you have a good chance of bumping into a genuine old fashioned 'bheestie' with his traditional twin goatskin water containers which he hawks round to his customers (all of whom will be Muslin as no Hindu will drink water 'contaminated' by animal skin).

Colin Lane leads east to where it meets Colin Street, close to the junction with Rafi Ahmed Kidwai Road (the old Wellesley Street). Before you reach this junction you will find, to your right, a series of tiny, unnamed and interconnecting gullees which first lead south, then join into a single by-lane going east and emerging close to the above junction. It is worthwhile spending a little time wandering these gullees which are typical of what much of the area would have been like about 150 years ago.

Where you emerge from the eastern end of these gullees, have a look to your right down Rafi Ahmed Kidwai Road. About 20 metres south there is a sort of pavement snack bar come chaikhana with benches for customers to sit. This is a favourite spot for the 'bheesties' operating in the area to take their refreshment. There is even a convenient iron grill at the back edge of the pavement on which the 'bheesties' hang their yoked goatskin water carriers whilst taking tiffin.

Turning back from the junction, follow Colin Street northwards until you come to the junction with Marquis Street. This stretch of the Street provides a good introduction to what lies beyond. It is usually thronged with people, hastening to and from who knows where, noisily engaged in pavement commerce, in loading and unloading merchandise from madly parked carriers or simply standing in groups gossiping, adding to the myriad obstacles for the pedestrian to negotiate.

Once past Marquis Street, Colin Street continues north and becomes, if anything even more congested but here there is an additional hazard; the speeding rickshaw puller. These are liable, without warning, to come hurtling out of the numerous narrow side lanes leading off this stretch of Colin Street. The majority will not be carrying passengers but goods, heaped precariously high, swaying alarmingly and threatening to spill out all over the road at every change of direction. Work on the principle that it is far easier for you to come to a stop or take avoiding action than it is for the rickshaw puller and all should go well.

About 50 metres on past the Marquis Street crossing, you will find Market Street off to your left. Amidst all the hubbub of the place, there is to be found a fair number of small butchers' shops with a good deal of the 'stock' in the form of chickens and goats caged or tethered outside the premises. The squeamish would do well not to loiter here for too long. Along the Street, the first turning on your right is Dukura Bagan where, about thirty metres north and off to your right, begins a very narrow, unnamed gullee. This opens out into a kind of tiny square before leading off westwards in four separate directions; another hidden little backwater seemingly caught in a time warp.

Back in Dukura Bagan, either of the first two turnings on your right, amusingly, both named Uma Das Lane, return you back into Colin Street. Turning right here, about 15 metres south and to your left, is the start of another narrow unnamed lane which leads straight through to Rafi Ahmed Kidwai Road. This lane is much used as a shortcut by busy rickshaw pullers in a hurry and it is therefore advisable to keep well to one side.

Where the lane emerges into Rafi Ahmed Kidwai Road, standing opposite is the great white painted edifice of the Lord Jesus Church. Built in 1848 by the Scottish Church, it was originally known as St. Margaret's and later Wellesley Square Church. From the 1960's it was taken over by Catholic Jesuits. Within, there is a splendid library much used for study purposes by local students.

Immediately outside the Church's noble railings there is an unofficial and therefore illegal collection of pavement shanties stretching southwards for more than 100 metres right to the junction with Hazi MD Mahsin Square (the old Wellesley

Square as proclaimed by an ancient and still surviving street nameplate). These shanties, constructed of the usual scavenged debris, have stood here for some years. The inhabitants, mainly Bangladeshi families, certainly appear established here and are seemingly well organised; there is even what looks remarkably like a kind of crèche operating at one of these structures and, at another, evidence of a communal 'laundry' facility.

One peculiarity of this stretch of Rafi Ahmed Kidwai Road is the seemingly ever present sewer clearing taking place. Nearly every time I have passed by there has been, at some point along this thoroughfare, a cordoned off area in the centre of the carriageway where a manhole has been lifted, and a gang of workmen are busily engaged in this activity. It may well be that, deep beneath this Road there is some complicated confluence of sewer pipers particularly prone to silting up or it may be simply that by age and design, the sewers are no longer able to cope with present day demands. Whatever the reason, the traveller on foot will come across similar scenes when strolling through the older areas of Calcutta and it is worth noting what the work involves.

Having wrestled the heavy iron manhole cover from its socket in the carriageway, one and sometimes two of the work gang armed with shovels, descend into the sewer, some two to three metres below. A large iron bucket is then lowered to them on a rope by other members of the gang above. Once the bucket is filled it is manually hauled to the surface and emptied onto the roadway gradually forming a large heap of what looks remarkably like black grease but which smells rather differently. None of the workmen have any visible safety equipment; those down in the sewer having no breathing equipment, face mask, safety harness or even gloves. When those below emerge back into the daylight you see that they are also barefoot. You have been standing watching all this for perhaps ten minutes. The temperature at street level is in the high 30's C.

with humidity around 98%. You have not been exerting your-self, are out in the open air but are by now feeling distinctly uncomfortable. Nevertheless, it requires a leap of the imagi-nation to put yourself in the place of those working in the air-less, stifling and foetid sewer below.

Just past the pavement settlement, turn left into Hazi MD Mahsin Square. To your right is the Calcutta Madrasa along whose boundary wall stretches another sprawling collection of pavement shanties, far grimmer and more forbidding than those you have just passed in Rafi Ahmed Kidwai Road. Again, the inhabitants are mainly Bangladeshi migrants.

As you continue eastwards, the thoroughfare becomes Deodar Bux Lane for the 150 metres or so until it ends at the junction with Taltola Lane. Turning right here the next turning to your left is Doctor Lane; one of four identically named lanes in this area, none of which have any apparent common link and all leading off in different directions. As confusing as the three similarly eccentrically scattered Durgan Charan Doctor Roads also located close by.

Some 100 metres east along this Doctor Lane and the third turning on your left, is the beginning of Taltala Bazar Street. This hugely busy and ancient thoroughfare is thick with small traders, shoppers and the inevitable groups of gossiping idlers. There are scores of rickshaws weaving their passengers or cargo through the throng whilst an equal number are parked up in the side lanes, their pullers snatching a rest from recent exertions. Along the Street is nearly always to be found a Chabbi Wallah plying his trade. Instantly recognisable by the large iron hoop of key blanks which he jangles to attract commissions, the Chabbi Wallah is in the business of key making. He (for I have never seen a female in this calling), works by eye alone. Show him your key and he will unroll his kit of files, select a blank from his hoop and in no time at all will have produced a perfect copy; true, old fashioned crafts-manship in action.

As you near the end of Taltala Bazar Street, you cross the junction with another of the previously mentioned, multiple Doctor Streets. Just past this junction the Street ends where it meets Surendra Nath (S.N.) Banerjee Road. This busy main thoroughfare links Mirza Ghalib Street to the west with A.P.C. Road to the east. As you head in the direction of A.P.C. Road, you will notice a number of very impressive, old residential buildings on both sides of the Road, many having magnificent shuttered balconies at first floor level. Sadly, a number appear to be in a very sorry state of repair and it is anyone's guess as to how long these fine buildings will survive. On the right hand side of the Road stands the Osmand Memorial Church. Formerly the Wesleyan Chapel, the building was constructed in 1868 to a specification which looks as if it was intended to last until doomsday.

A little further east, off the opposite (northern) side of the Road, is Waverly Lane, once known locally as 'Pudding Lane' by reason of the highly regarded fresh puddings which were produced here daily up until the 1950's. This short Lane leads through to Dharmatala Street, now officially renamed Lenin Sarani. This also marks the northern boundary of Taltala and beginning of Muchipara, one of the most densely populated parts of Calcutta. Muchipara sprawls northwards from here right up to Surya Sen Street.

Turn left into Lenin Sarani and walking westwards, take the first turning on your right, just past the Red Church. This is Beni Mullick Lane which 20 metres or so on, crosses Creek Row and becomes Mohendra Sarkar Street. The large building to the right at this junction is the Metropolitan Institute School, one of a number of schools and colleges located here-abouts. Mohendra Sarkar Street performs a 90 degree left turn about mid-way along its length before reaching the junction with Sashi Bhusan Dey Street. Just before this junction, on the right hand side of the Street, is Matri Bhandar, an ancient and popular grocery store, famous locally for stocking the most obscure things.

You can also find at this junction a number of Aakh Wallahs and their ingenious machines. The Aakh Wallah is the chap who operates the sugar cane presses you will see all over Calcutta. The press looks rather like the old fashioned clothes mangle complete with giant cogs and rollers. The lengths of raw cane are fed through the machine by turning a large wheeled handle and are crushed between cogs and rollers to extract the cloudy, sweet white juice which is drunk for its refreshing, energy giving qualities. The machines are magnificent pieces of engineering, so finely worked that one swing of the wheeled handle will set the apparatus in motion for a minute or more. Nearly all have a bell attached to the handle which, in rotation, tinkles a warning to stand clear as the cogs and rollers are in motion.

Sashi Bhusan Dey Street is the central main thoroughfare of this southern half of Muchipara. This busy and hectic artery is crammed full of life along its entire length northwards until it spills out into B.B. Ganguly Street. The first turning on your right is Serpentine Lane which squiggles like its namesake northwards to join Santosh Mitra Square. This ancient Lane contains some very fine old residential buildings of late 18th and early 19th century origin. Confusingly, there are three other thoroughfares called Serpentine Lane within a stone's throw of this location. None of these now seems to bear any obvious connection to each other and is possibly another example of an ancient, once continuous thoroughfare becoming fragmented and scattered about as a result of subsequent development.

At the end of this particular Serpentine Lane, turn left and you will rejoin Sashi Bhusan Dey Street almost opposite the junction with Ram Nath Kabiraj Lane. Just north of this point, along the eastern side of the Street and just past the small Lebutala Bazar, a by-lane off to the right leads through to the Lebutala Bustee area. This collection of overcrowded slum dwellings is mainly occupied by poor Bihari families, seemingly engaged in scavenging judging by the piles of empty plastic bottles, old bicycle tyres, scrap tin and the like piled about everywhere.

Back in Sashi Bhusen Dey Street, cross over to the western pavement and adjacent to the Railway Co-operative Bank, you will find Billa's Chow Shop, a famous eatery of the area and highly recommended.

Continuing northwards along Sashi Bhusen Dey Street, the next turning on your left is the eastern end of the ancient Hideram Banerji Lane This gracefully curving Lane stretches westwards all the way to join College Street, at the point where the latter becomes Nirmal Chandra Street. The Lane is widely used by pedestrians making to and from Sealdah Station as an alternative to congested and less easily walkable, B.B. Ganguly Street. The Lane contains many very old residential buildings, some dating to the late 18th century and prime for listing as heritage buildings.

The lanes leading off both north and south from Hideram Banerji Lane are also of historic significance. Take the small unnamed by-lane, being the first turning on your right and this leads into Sil Lane. As you walk westwards along this Lane, which is surrounded by bustees, the first turning to your right is Ram Kanai Adhikari Lane. This historic Lane which links through to B.B. Ganguly Street was once called St. James' Lane and long before that, Scavengers Lane. The fourth turning on your left off Hideram Banerji Lane is Panchannantala Lane where the great 19th century social reformer and educationalist, Ishwardchandra Vidyasagar (1820 – 1891), lived when he first came to Calcutta.

Almost opposite Panchannantala Lane, off the northern side of Hideram Banerji Lane, is Durga Pituri Lane. This Lane contains a number of mid 18th century buildings which, as with many of the other buildings in this locality are really deserving of conservation. The northern end of this Lane meets B.B. Ganguly Street, less than 100 metres east of the Bow Bazar/College Street Crossing; in the geometric sense, the very epicentre of Calcutta proper.

Walk westwards along B.B. Ganguly Street and just past the junction with College Street, off the northern pavement, is an open fronted Hindu Shrine of unusual origin. This is the 'Firinghee Kali Bari', the foreigner's temple of Kali Ma. The foreigner was the builder of the temple, an unusual 19th century Englishman called Anthony Kabial. He joins those such as the wonderful 'Hindoo Stuart' as amongst the few westerners of the age to fully embrace the Hindu religion and culture.

A few minutes walk west of Anthony Kabiel's legacy you reach the junction with Chitteranjan Avenue and the location of Central metro station.

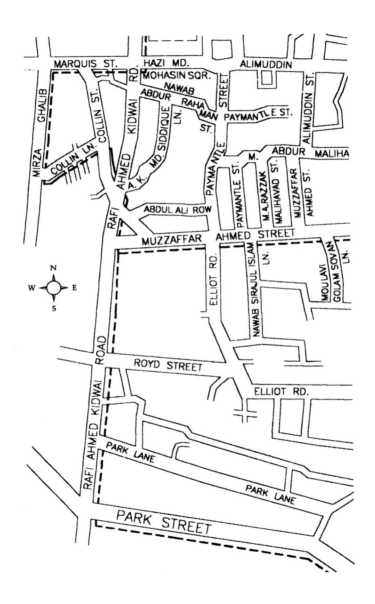

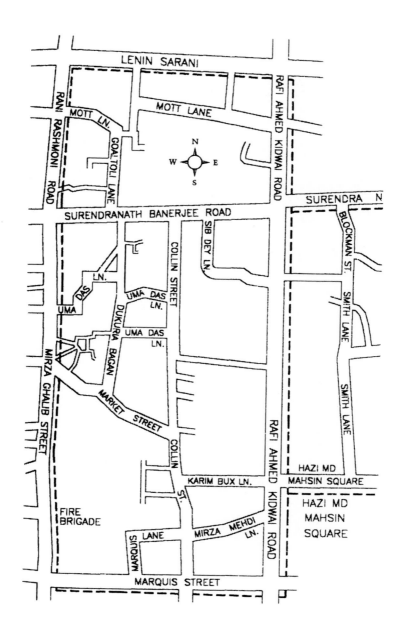

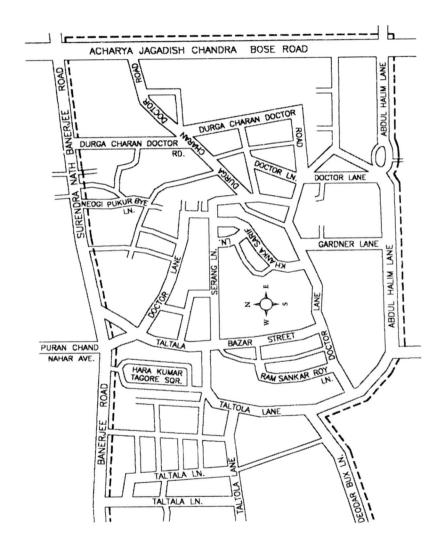

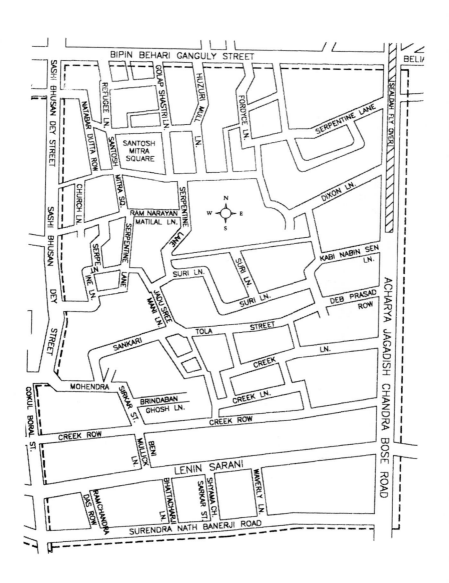

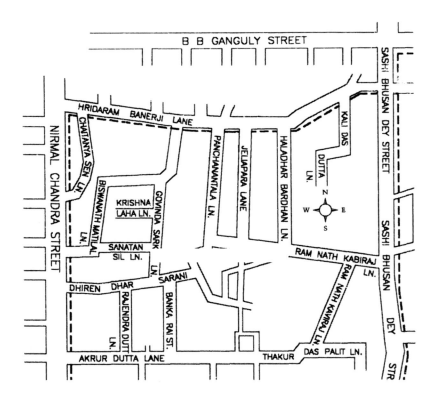

CHAPTER 11

Howrah Railway Station

Seen from a distance the great redbrick structure of Howrah Railway Station could quite easily be mistaken for a great palace or some monumental fortification. Indeed this latter possibility is not so far off the mark since the British tended to build Indian railway stations with at least one eye on their ease of defence should the need arise.

No trip to Calcutta is complete without a visit to this great terminus on the west bank of the Hooghly, almost within the shadow of the Howrah Bridge. Howrah Station is one of the largest railway complexes in India and almost certainly the busiest.

The nearest metro station to Howrah Railway Station is Mahatma Ghandi (M.G.) Road, a good 30 to 40 minute walk east. Whilst trams no longer cross the Howrah Bridge to serve the station, trams nos. 11, 20, 21, 26 and 30 all run along M.G. Road and terminate at the eastern approach to the Howrah Bridge. From there simply cross the Bridge and the Station is located to your left; the several hundred taxis parked in front being an aid to navigation.

The first rail line from Calcutta was laid in 1854 and ran from Howrah, then a small town, northwest to the coalfields in the Bardhaman district of Bengal. This was only the second railway line in the whole sub-continent; the first being laid a year earlier from Bombay (Mumbai) to Thaney. The line from Howrah, a single track affair carried goods trains only. The original station comprising little more than a wooden shed adjoining a number of godowns was replaced in a few years by a colonnaded building, which remained in use right up to the end of the 19th century.

The present main station at Howrah was completed in 1905 to a design by the British railway engineer Halsey Ricardo. The station had 13 tracks later extended to 21 with plans on the drawing board to increase this to 37. In the 1980's the station was extended with a new complex just south of the main building.

Trains from Howrah serve the greater Calcutta urban area, the whole of West Bengal State and most major cities in India. A number of India's most important trunk rail routes end at Howrah. The Station handles more than 400 train movements every day.

Railway stations the world over, being hubs of human transit, tend to be crowded and busy places; so too is Howrah but on a scale which almost defies belief. Once inside the station, it is as if half the populace of Calcutta has arrived ahead of you and is either boarding or waiting for outgoing trains while the other half is streaming off those which have just arrived. To get some idea of the scale of human movement taking place, you need to find some vantage point from where you are in sight of the platform barriers without fear of being trampled to death in the melee swirling everywhere about you. Once an incoming train grinds metallically to a halt, and often before that, doors are flung open and the platform is instantly swarmed with alighting passengers, pressing forward in a seemingly never ending stream, flowing through the barriers out into the concourse and through the pedestrian underpass and station exits, meeting equal numbers coming the other way. Amidst this contraflow of humanity there are sitting, or laying all over the Station concourse at any hour of the day or night, hundreds of waiting passengers, singly or in whole family groups with their amorphous bundles of possessions bound up tightly in rope or anything else suitable which was to hand. Some are sleeping, some gossiping or eating, others simply waiting with that fatalistic patience rarely witnessed outside India. It has been estimated that upwards of 2.5 million people pass through the Station every day.

Weaving amongst this human maelstrom are the knowledgeable and indispensible station coolies with their brass licence badges and red, green or orange workshirts. One glance at your ticket and they are off with your luggage held aloft, expertly guiding you through the throng to the correct platform, the right train and even to the right carriage.

The chorus of porters, hawkers and passengers, of trains arriving and departing, of garbled announcements through battered loudspeakers all contribute to the general level of mixed din within the Station. Nobody talks at Howrah; everyone shouts, they must if they are to be heard by their neighbour.

Within the station are scores of outlets where you can buy anything from hot and cold drinks, fresh fruit, newspapers, posters and badges of Hindu deities, and all the provisions you may need for journey to the other end of the sub-continent. Here you can have your shoes mended and cleaned, your face shaved, hair cut and sometimes there is even present a man who for a small fee, will iron your clothes.

There are some wonderful signs of admonition prominently displayed along the concourse. 'Ticketless travel is a social evil and crime' is one of my favourites, so too is 'Cleanliness is next to Godliness'.

On almost any day you can see people from all over the sub-continent passing through Howrah. Malayalees and Tamils from the deep south en route to or from Madras, Maduri, Trivandrum and Cochin; those from the north eastern States of Assam, Meghalaya, Manipur and Tripura; Biharis and Oriyas from neighbouring states and those from further afield, from Gujarat, Punjab Maharashtra and even Kashmir.

The Station and its environs has, almost from the day it was laid out, also played host to refugees, the homeless, the other-wise rootless and dispossessed, and new arrivals to the City, fleeing poverty, debt, the arm of the law or their families. In the early 1980's there were still scores of families, refugees from the mayhem preceding the founding of Bangladesh,[7] still living camped out on the platforms of Howrah, more than a decade after the conflict from which they had fled; some of their children having been born there, never having known any other home.

Today by far the largest and most socially disturbing group of Station denizens are the tribes of semi-feral children who wind up here from Calcutta's streets, the hinterland of Bengal and locations far beyond; forming themselves into tight knit clans for mutual protection and survival. The railway police, the Railway Protection Force (RPF), estimate that the Station complex now provides a home for up to 3.000 of these chil-dren, living between and beneath the platforms, along the tracks and in the numerous sidings under decaying goods wagons. The overwhelming majority are boys but girls too also feature in these tribes. Some have gravitated to Howrah follow-ing an earlier career of joyriding India's rail network; many of these are amazingly well travelled. Others have been aban-doned, lost or have fled abusive or violent homes; a percentage will have drifted here after having been abducted.

---

[7]See Annexe 1 - Historical Notes

They live on their wits and by scavenging and pilfering in and around the station and on every incoming train. Before arriving trains have even come to a stop, gangs of these children will descend like a biblical plague of locusts, carrying off almost anything discarded by passengers, empty plastic water bottles, newspapers and half eaten food. They will also carry off anything which unwary or distracted passengers have not kept a very firm grip upon; wallets, purses, handbags, briefcases, cell phones, anything which can be sold or traded. It is instructive to hang around the Railway Protection Force booth, located in the middle of the station concourse, to listen to the litany of voluble complaints from disgruntled passengers who have just been relieved of their personal property by these mini bandits. The inexperienced western traveller is particularly vulnerable, not least because of their possible unwillingness to recognise the very real risk children of such tender years can pose in this environment.

The greater number of these children are solvent abusers; the nauseating smell of glue being present everywhere they congregate; the other clue being their constant sniffing from old socks or rags impregnated with the stuff. 'Denrite', a glue, seems to be the current solvent of choice. Some of the 'older' ones, which generally means those above about 12 years of age, have other drug dependency problems, including heroin addiction. This widespread dependency is the means by which many of the children have been ensnared by the 'dadas', the adult gangster ringleaders of these child gangs, who use the children as thieves or couriers of drugs and other contraband, including firearms. These 'dadas' base themselves outside the station, in the surrounding slums and bars of Howrah and along the nearby west bank of the Hooghly, outside the reach of the Railway Protection Force. Many of these 'dadas' were formerly just like the station children they now control, having risen through the ranks as it were. Amongst their number are some very nasty characters indeed, involved in every sphere of criminal activity from receiving stolen goods, drug dealing and vice to extortion and contract killing. These types feature regularly in the wanted lists published by the Calcutta Police which you can inspect at any of the City's police stations.

There is little sympathy apparent for these children from locals and others regularly using Howrah Station; understandable perhaps since these are the very people most directly affected by the many predations of these wild bands. These station children are not entirely abandoned by society; there are a number of voluntary organisations concerned for their welfare. One such is SEED (the Society for Educational and Environmental Development). Founded in 1991 for the development of the slum dwellers of Howrah generally, for the last decade the Society has worked with children on the streets and in the station. SEED runs a drop in centre located just outside the station, and two safe night shelters; one for girls and one for boys, nearby. The Society also organises 'platform schools', teaching basic literacy and numeracy skills and engaging with the children.

Approximately 300 metres south of the main station building is a, as yet unpublicised gem; the Eastern Railway Museum. This Museum was opened in 2006 and is only the second of its kind in the whole sub-continent, the other being in Delhi. The Museum houses examples of old and rare steam and electric locomotives, exhibitions of photographs tracing the history of railways in eastern India together with various artefacts and models recording the evolution of signalling and track laying. There is also a superb model of the Howrah Station complex.

The Museum is in a park like setting, complete with fountain and a working miniture train to keep younger charges amused. The Museum is open every day, except Thursdays, between 1.00 pm and 8.00 pm, admission is 5 Rupees plus a further 10 Rupees if you fancy a ride on the miniture train.

CHAPTER 12

South Park Street Cemetery

This is not so much a walk but more in the way of a pilgrimage to an Imperial necropolis which is the last resting place of many of the earliest British inhabitants of Calcutta. Here in shaded groves amongst sepulchral obelisks, urns, pyramids, catalfaques and other funereal and lichen encrusted, memorials lie many of the once great and the good, those of rank and importance. Here too are interred many of the less exulted; the civil and military servants of the East India Company, the merchants, the professional classes along with their wives and children; all, in their different ways, contributors to the early development of Calcutta from a muddy trading outpost into a great City.

The South Park Street Cemetery is sited at the south western corner of the junction of Park Street with A.J.C. Bose Road; an approximate 20 minute walk southwards down Park Street from the metro station of that name. There was once another old cemetery located immediately opposite on the northern side of Park Street. The site of this other cemetery is now occupied by the Assembly of God Church, the Mission of Mercy Hospital and the Apeejay School. There is just one memorial still remaining from this long obliterated cemetery and this can be found, set incongruously just to the right of the side of the Hospital facing Park Street. This single monument is the Robertson memorial bearing the details of six members of that family, one of whom was a Commissioner of the Calcutta Police and another, a Senior Superintendent of that force.

The South Park Street Cemetery or the 'Great Cemetery' as it was originally known is now administered by the Christian Burial Board of Calcutta. The Cemetery was opened on 25th August 1767 with the first recorded burial being that of one John Wood, a writer of the Customs House. In those early days the site of the Cemetery occupied marshy, forested terrain and was approached by a bund, later to become known as Burial Ground Road. Burials would take place after dark by lantern light. The only burials to take place outside the hours of darkness were military funerals which were accompanied by rolling guns.

Through the main gate, you enter a large portico which houses the offices of the Cemetery Superintendent and the surviving archives which comprise an alphabetical list of surnames cross referenced to grave numbers. These archives can be made available for inspection upon request. When you enter you will be asked to sign the visitors' book; which also contains space to add your comments on your way out. Through this portico is the main pathway into the Cemetery, with some of the oldest graves being those closest to the entrance.

What most strikes the first time visitor is the haunting, decaying grandeur of the place; the fantastic architecture of death celebrated with neo-classical mausoleums, Egyptian inspired pyramid tombs, columns, arches, and domed, temple like monuments, much of it executed on a grand scale. There can be scarcely a still upright original monument anywhere here standing less than elbow level and much that is two or three times the height of the average man. All of this engraved with the once fashionable symbols of mortality; crossed cannon, anchors, swords, hour glasses, skulls, scythes and such like.

Then there is the inescapable sensation of tranquillity. It is difficult to believe that Calcutta is going full belt only just outside the high boundary walls. The calm serenity of this tree shaded oasis lends much to the sombre and ghostly atmosphere pervading the entire place.

Rudyard Kipling, never a fan of Calcutta generally, was equally scathing about the Cemetery. He wrote, in his 1888 work, 'City of Dreadful Night', 'The tombs are small houses. It is as though we walked down the streets of a town, so tall are they and so closely do they stand – a town shrivelled by fire, and scared by frost and siege. Men must have been afraid of their friends rising up before the due time that they weighted them down with such cruel mounds of masonry.' Lucia Palk, the heroine of the final chapter of this work, 'Concerning Lucia', is buried here. The inscription on her tomb reads; 'Lucia, wife of Robert Palk. Daughter of Rev. Dr. Stonehouse, Born Northampton 26th November 1747 Deceased 22nd June 1772.' This is followed by twenty lines of verse ending with;

> 'The grief will weep and friendship heave the sigh;
> Tho wounded memory, the fond tear shall shed;
> Yet let no fruitless sorrow dim the eye;
> To teach the living, lie the sacred dead.'

The mortality rate amongst those early inhabitants of Calcutta was dreadful: two monsoons being the popularly estimated life span of new arrivals from the west. The inhospitable climate, malaria and other tropical diseases took a fearful toll as did childbirth, poor sanitation and the primitive medical care available. Children and infants were particularly vulnerable as many of the memorial inscriptions testify. 'Susannah Hunter deceased 7th October 1792 aged 29 years and three of her children who all died in infancy' is typical. Similarly, 'Catherine Sykes deceased 28th December 1786 aged 23 years and her stillborn child' or 'Ann Hayes deceased 29th December 1803

aged 24 years and two of her infant children', being sadly typical examples.

Conversely, there are some surprising examples of longevity
against all the odds. 'Dr Roland Jackson resident here for
32 years, died 29th March 1784 having attained 63 years'

Others were not so lucky, 'Augustus Cleveland, late Collector
of Revenues died 12th January 1784 aged 29 whilst at sea on
route to the Cape for the recovery of his health'. He is amongst
the many recorded as, having survived the rigours of Calcutta,
being cruelly snatched away whilst on route home or to a place
of recovery.

Perhaps the tallest monument in the Cemetery is the dazzlingly
whitewashed pyramid tomb of Sir William Jones, founder of
the Royal Asiatic Society of Bengal. This learned Society, now
minus the Royal prefix, survives to this day, housed at the other
end of Park Street, near to the junction with Chowringhee.
He came to Calcutta in 1783 as a judge of the Supreme Court.
A man of formidable intellect, he was the pioneer of modern
Indian studies, making the first English translations of numerous important works of Indian literature. He died on 27th April
1794 aged just 47 years. The upkeep of his tomb has been
funded ever since by the Society he founded.

A close rival, in terms of size, is the tomb (also in the form of a
pyramid) of Elizabeth Jane Barwell 'The Celebrated Miss
Sanderson' as the inscription reads. She is known to have
arrived in Calcutta in 1775 and was quickly acclaimed the society beauty of her day; the belle of Calcutta's grand balls. She
had numerous suitors seeking her hand and eventually married
Richard Barwell, Calcutta born and bred. He was a member of
the Council of the Presidency under Warren Hastings' Governor Generalship and the sole supporter of the latter on that
body. He was also a notorious rake and gambler. Within two

years of her marriage, weakened by childbirth and fever, she died on 9th November, 1778 'aged about 23'.

Nearby, is the tomb of General Clavering, another member of the Presidency Council under Warren Hastings and his implacable opponent, constantly plotting the downfall of the Governor General.

Here too rests the mortal remains of Lady Anne Monson, the wife of The Hon. Colonel Monson, yet another member of Hastings' Presidency Council and a great granddaughter of King Charles II. Warren Hastings was amongst the pall bearers of her coffin to the Cemetery Gates where it was handed over to 'six ladies of noble birth' who bore it the rest of the way to the grave.

Possibly the most unique tomb, taking the form of a Hindu temple with stone carvings of the Goddess Ganga, is that of the madly and wonderfully eccentric, Major General Charles Stuart or 'Hindoo Stuart' as he became most widely known. Born in 1758 Stuart came to India in his teens as an army cadet. He was to stay in India for the rest of his life, rising through the ranks to Major General. He was one of the very few British officers to wholeheartedly embrace the Hindu religion and culture, having, in the words of a contemporary commentator, 'enthusiastically studied the language, manners and customs of the natives of the country'. He quickly adopted many Indian customs including bathing in the Hughli every morning, taking Paan and wearing Indian clothing.

Stuart was a frequent letter writer to the Calcutta Telegraph newspaper, encouraging European ladies to adopt the sari; a suggestion which, in the opening years of the 19th century, must have been considered outrageous to many of those at which it was directed. He subsequently published his letters and some of the responses from the less amused readers in a superb volume exhaustively entitled 'The Ladies' Monitor, Being a Series of Letters First Published in Bengal On The Subject of Female Apparel Tending to Favour a regulated adoption of Indian Costume And a rejection of Superfluous Vesture By the ladies of this Country With Incidental remarks on Hindoo Beauty, Whale Bone Stays, Iron Busks, Indian Corsets, Man-Milliners, Idle Bachelors, Hair Powder, Waiting Maids and Footmen'. Among the reasons he put forward for European ladies to abandon their iron busks was that it made the wearers more susceptible to lightening strikes. Perhaps he had a point since a small but nevertheless surprising number of those buried here are recorded as having been struck down during electrical storms.

He amassed a considerable collection of sculptures and other idols of Hindu deities which he had sent to England to form the basis of the British Museum's oriental collection.

Perhaps the most amazing thing is that Stuart's eccentricity and outspokenness, given the accepted norms of the age, does not appear to have had any adverse effect upon his career. Today, much of what he believed and forcefully propounded would be considered by many to be evidence of an enlightened mind. What the stiffer elements of his own time made of him can only be imagined.

'Hindoo Stuart' died on the last day of March 1828. The fact that he is buried in this Christian cemetery is perhaps proof that he did not entirely abandon the religion of his birth. But perhaps this in itself represents his last elaborate challenge to the conventions of the day; after all he lies beneath a replica of a Hindu temple, having been buried along with some of the idols of deities of that religion.

Sons of Charles Dickens and Captain Cook are interred here; so too is William Thackeray's father. Others include Henry

Chastaney, one time private secretary to Warren Hastings and Lt. Col. Robert Kyd the distinguished botanist who founded Calcutta's famous Botanical Gardens, located a few kilometres downriver from the Howrah Bridge.

Also buried here is Rose Aylmer, fleetingly the teenaged inamorata of the poet Walter Savage Landor. Within a year of her arrival in Calcutta she succumbed to cholera in the outbreak of 1800, aged just 20 years. Landor was devastated at her death, composing a poem in her memory, the following part of which, in 1910, was inscribed at the base of the graceful, spiral fluted column which marks her tomb:

> 'Ah what awaits the sceptred race!
> Ah, what the form divine!
> What every virtue, every grace
> Rose Aylmer, all were thine...'

Quite close by the tomb of 'Hindoo Stuart' is the comparatively modest grave of Henry Vivian Louis Derozio, the young Anglo Indian poet, radical and inspiration behind the Young Bengal Movement of the early years of the 19th century. He is said to have been heavily influenced by the social and political ideals behind the French Revolution with which he sought to enthuse the pupils he taught at Calcutta's Hindu College. For this he was accused of trying to spread atheism and was dismissed from his post. He died shortly after at the very young age of 22 years. The maintenance of his grave is funded to this day by the Anglo Indian Association of Calcutta.

It is very easy to spend several hours wandering the Cemetery, immersed in everything about you. First time visitors often remark on the level of decay affecting many of the monuments; two and a half centuries of Calcutta's climate having obliterated many inscriptions and given a moth eaten appearance to many monuments by exposing areas of the underlying brick structure. Up until a few decades ago it was all very much more derelict, with squatters untidily occupying any vacant space and pariah dogs and even cows nosing about between the monuments. The Christian Burial Board has brought about huge improvements to the Cemetery with much sympathetic restoration to the monuments having been undertaken and a great deal more in progress. Most of the collapsed headstones have now been reset either vertically in the boundary walls or horizontally along pathways. Given the limited financial and manpower resources available to the Board its achievements have been remarkable.

There is quite nearby this Cemetery, two others used over the years for Christian burials but neither is anywhere near the same stamp as South Park Street.

The first of these cemeteries is the General Episcopal Cemetery but is more generally known as the Lower Circular Road (the old name for A.J.C. Bose Road) Cemetery. This is to be found north of the South Park Street Cemetery along the eastern side of A.J.C. Bose Road, just before the sprawling Beniapukur Tram Depot. This Cemetery is still in use and the front part nearest to A.J.C. Bose Road, is relatively clear and reasonably well kept. The older graves are to be found further east and around the perimeter of the grounds. These areas are in a de-plorable condition; so badly overgrown that graves without vertically raised gravestones or monuments are no longer vis-ible. The Cemetery does have rudimentary records of the older graves but these do not stretch back further than the late 1930's. The cemetery staff are helpful and will if asked (and for a modest consideration), use crowbars to prise back the creepers to allow inspection of any of the graves swamped by undergrowth.

The second cemetery is the Scottish Cemetery, still proudly proclaimed in an arched ironwork nameplate above the main entrance. This old, walled Cemetery has not been in use for well over half a century and is now rarely visited. It can be found east of the South Park Street Cemetery, sandwiched between Park Street and the eastern end of Shakespeare Sarani and occupying the area of land between Karaya Road and Mrigendra Lal Mitra Road. The iron entrance gates are generally padlocked but give them a good rattle to alert the resident caretaker and he will let you in. Once inside the decay is immediately apparent. There are toppled or drunkenly leaning headstones and monuments everywhere and areas so overgrown that you cannot see the graves until you are standing right on top of them. There are other monuments still standing proudly erect, many marking family tombs of the 19th century. Amidst all this apparent neglect there is clear evidence that some attempt is regularly made to prevent the Cemetery grounds from reverting entirely to jungle. So far as I could ascertain, there is only the caretaker and one old gardener to do this and although they strive as best they can, the task is quite beyond such slim resources. The caretaker keeps some interment records which can be consulted and the inevitable visitors' book which he will invite you to sign and add your comments.

Epilogue

Calcutta Night

The Calcutta of the darkness hours is a place where the once familiar assumes new guises, where the side-streets and lanes lay camouflaged in caverns of deepening shadow set between pockets of flickering light from oil lamps, the dull glow of single, bare electric bulbs or the stark jarring coldness of the occasional unshaded neon tube. It is where the traveller can literally, stumble on the unexpected unless extra care is taken when navigating the gloomier recesses. It becomes a place of shuttered shop-fronts, of doorways barred by over padlocked grills or guarded by uniformed chowkidars with their plastic chair or wooden stool to provide rudimentary repose during their night long vigils.

Long after the sun has set Calcutta continues to heave; pulsating with an energy which is not yet quite spent for the day. The closing of the Calcutta day is attended by the same frenetic activity which heralds its beginning. The same battered buses, crammed full to bursting with those who have a home to go to will be grinding up and down Chitteranjan Avenue, along M.G. Road and back and forth through the other central thoroughfares, trailing in their wake clouds of diesel exhaust made more visible in the headlights of following traffic. Similarly overflowing trams will still be scraping along their tracks, sparks flashing brightly in the darkness from their electric motors, emitting a metallic screech of protest as they brake to a stop to set down and replenish their human cargoes.

Open backed lorries, jammed full with casual building workers, standing sentinels shouldering spades, picks and other
tools of their calling, will be stopping at junctions, offloading
different work gangs from where they were collected earlier in
the day and from where the luckier ones will again be departing at next sunrise.

The rickshaw pullers will still be much in evidence whilst
commissions are still to be had, many, at this end of the evening,
transporting goods rather than passengers. In movement they
take on the appearance of the flickering antiquated film clip as
they move rapidly between the lighted spots and shadow, the
spokes of the rapidly revolving wheels appearing motionless by
trick of the light. Others, whose long day has ended, are heading off towards their rickshaw garages at Giribabu Lane in Bow
Bazar, Serpantine Lane further east near Sealdah and other
depots dotted about the City. Some, whose rickshaw doubles as
their sleeping quarters, will be making their way to their usual
night time stopovers along Calcutta's side-streets and lanes.

The metro stations dotted along the City's north-south spine
continue to disgorge their streams of commuters, from the
brightly lit platforms below to the more dimly illuminated
areas at street level. Within the next half hour these streams will
begin to dwindle and finally become a trickle as the system
winds down for the day and the last trains pass through, heading for the termini at Dum Dum to the north and Tollygunge to
the south.

The darkness hours are a time when the traveller from the west
may wander abroad through Calcutta's dimly lit byways enjoy-
ing a sense of anonymity unachievable in daylight. For now it is
only at close quarters and in a favourable light that their difference from those amongst who they walk may be determined. It
is a good time to loiter in apparent idleness, taking in all that is
going on about you. Like the family of pavement sleepers

spreading their blankets, staking out their pitch by carefully positioning their meagre possessions, the children still young enough to think it all a great adventure. The elderly beggar lady, her thin body twisted by affliction or trickery, removing the accumulation of coins from her tin bowl, secreting them amongst the folds of her ragged clothing, for fear she appear a less meritorious case for charity. The small group of loafers, squatting in a tight circle around an upturned crate, volubly engaged in some incomprehensible card game of chance.

An hour or so remains until the still thronged streets and lanes will begin to thin and the discordant orchestra of mechanical and human clamour subside. In Beadon Street followers of the dramatic arts will by now be emerging from the brightly lit oasis that is the Minerva Theatre; affluent, well dressed people thronging the pavement and chatting excitedly about the night's performance, before being whisked off in their cars and taxis, perhaps to the fashionable restaurants of Park Street for late supper before returning to Salt Lake, Alipore or any of Calcutta's other desirable residential neighbourhoods.

Almost within spitting distance north of the Minerva, the less well heeled will be seeking another form of entertainment amongst the darkened twisting and crowded lanes of Sonagachi. Here several thousand sex workers nightly operate from the crumbling, decaying buildings which line the district's byways. It is a place which comes into being in the darkness hours and grows busier as the night wears on. Lines of impassive, heavily painted faces, with what dim light there is dully reflecting off lipstick, bangles and the other adornments necessary to the calling. Nervous young men, hoping to appear as if present by accident rather than design, furtively eyeing the ladies, seemingly both exited and repelled at the prospect of sinful adventure. Others swaggering, smelling strongly of the rough liquor whose effect has released enough inhibitions to drive them here in search of brief comfort of a kind.

Undisguised by the searing sunlight of day, the night streets of the City are wreathed in a vague opaqueness of smoke from the myriad charcoal and dung cooking fires, providing pinpricks of firelight in the darkened recesses wherever the eye is cast.

The traveller still here to witness the nights of late March and April, will sometimes experience the blue-white electrical discharges of lightening which, for a split second turn the whole sky brighter than daylight holding surrounding buildings in dark silhouette against the blinding backdrop and seemingly to hold all movement fleetingly motionless.

With the buses and trams departed to their depots for the night and traffic reduced to the odd roaming taxi and homebound bicycle, the near deserted streets assume a brief and uncharacteristic peacefulness. The traveller should make the most of it for such relative tranquillity will be short lived.

Annexe 1

Historical Notes

Footnote 1 - The Fall of Calcutta, 1756:

In little more than the half century or so since Job Charnock had established a permanent trading base for the East India Company on the east bank of the River Hooghly, Calcutta had grown from a loose collection of three small villages, (Sutanuti, Kalikata and Gobindapur), into a commercial and trading centre of considerable importance.

Fort William had been built in the first decade of the eighteenth century; an imposing fortification incorporating the Governor's house, the Company's warehouses and housing the servants, both military and civil. The Fort was at the heart of what was known as 'White Town' where the Europeans lived. By 1750 the City had grown to the extent that the mansions of 'White Town' stretched for more than a two kilometres along the east bank of the Hooghly and almost a kilometre inland. To the north and to the east of 'White Town' lay the sprawling, jumbled confusion of mud and reed huts housing Calcutta's teeming native population and extending the City's north/south boundaries to almost five kilometres.

The British were not the only Europeans trading in Bengal at this time; the Dutch, French and Portuguese all having their separate trading centres strung out at various points along the Hooghly. Trade by the British however, far exceeded that of all the other European interests put together.

The East India Company had been granted important conces-
sions by the Mughal Emperors in Delhi. The Company made
its own laws, marshalled its own military and police forces and,
initially, enjoyed immunity from taxation. The Company
nevertheless, relied heavily on maintaining the co-operation or
at the very least the acquiescence of the Nawabs, the rulers of
the Kingdom of Bengal. Although in theory, subservient to the
Emperors in Delhi, the Court of the Nawab of Bengal, based in
Murshidabad, some 230 kilometres to the north of Calcutta,
had become all powerful in the region. This came about largely
as a result of the great wealth generated by the lucrative trading of the Company and other European interests, a share of
which accrued to the Nawab and his Court.

For decades the attitude of the Nawabs had been one of self-
interested tolerance of the Company and the other European
trading concerns. The ageing Nawab, Alverdi Khan, compar-
ing the British to a hive of bees, summed up this attitude thus,
'of whose honey you might reap benefit but if you disturbed
their hive they would sting you to death'. It was Alverdi Khan
who had allowed the Company to construct the Maratha Ditch
as the eastern defence for Calcutta against the warlike,
marauding Marathas. His court had for many years suffered
the predations of the Marathas and he fully understood the
Company's need to protect their Calcutta trading base.

Alverdi Khan died in 1756 and was succeeded as Nawab by his
27 year old grandson, Siraj ud-Daula. This heralded a dramatic
change in policy towards the European traders and the East
India Company in particular. The new Nawab distrusted all
foreigners, particularly the British and was determined to rid
Bengal of their presence, by force if necessary.

If Siraj ud-Daula was, as contemporary accounts suggest, a
headstrong, impetuous and arrogant ruler, he was more than
matched in these negative qualities by the Governor of

Calcutta, Roger Drake. He was actually the Acting Governor, his appointment having yet to be confirmed by the Company's London headquarters (ironically such notification was only to reach Calcutta after the City's fall).

Only a few years older than the new Nawab, Drake was held by contemporaries to be pompous and vain and incapable of accepting advice from any quarter, including the other members of Calcutta's Governing Council. Perhaps because they shared such similarities of character, there existed between the Nawab and the Governor an undercurrent of mutual hatred and distrust.

A less arrogant and more astute Governor than Drake would have foreseen where matters were heading and would have employed diplomacy and tact to prevent the ongoing quarrels with the Nawab degenerating into open warfare. Drake took no such action and thereby played into the Nawab's hands. The Nawab, determined to seize Calcutta, employed two pretexts to launch hostilities.

The first pretext centred on the asylum given by the Governor to Kissendass, the son of the Nawab's Aunt (and eldest daughter of the late Alivardi) and therefore a potential rival for the Bengal throne. Kissendass had sensed the danger his contender status placed him in and had fled the Nawab's court for the sanctuary of Calcutta.

The Governor's subsequent stubborn refusal to expel Kissendass was viewed by the Nawab as part of a larger plot being hatched by the Company to help his rival unseat him from the throne.

The second pretext for warfare was an equally erroneous fear relating to a perceived strengthening of the fortifications of the European trading posts. These minor works were actually simply a precautionary measure by both the British and the French who at this time were engaged in hostilities with each other in Europe. Ever suspicious, the Nawab demanded that any new fortifications be dismantled immediately. The French replied diplomatically that they had built no new fortifications, only repaired one bastion which had been damaged by lightening strike; a response accepted by the Nawab. Governor Drake however, displayed no such tact and sent a provocative letter to the Nawab insisting on the right of the British to protect themselves in Calcutta against possible attack by the French, the implication being, even if unintended, that the Nawab was incapable of maintaining peace and order in his own kingdom. The Nawab's angry response, delivered at the end of May, 1756 amounted to a declaration of war.

Hostilities were not long delayed. At the beginning of June, the Nawab's army, variously estimated at fifty thousand strong, surrounded the Company's fort at Cossimbazar, just south of Murshidabad. Within a few days the fort, manned by a small garrison of less than 50 men, had surrendered without a shot being fired, leaving the Nawab's army free to march on to Calcutta.

It was only when news of the capture of Cossimbazar and the onward march of the Nawab's army reached Calcutta that the Governor, Members of the Council and the Garrison Commanders were shaken from their complacency into consternation and alarm. If ever there was a time requiring firm and decisive leadership, this was it. Governor Drake was not the man to provide it and even less so the garrison commander, Captain Commandant George Minchin.

It was only now that anyone thought to inspect the Fort's defences. These were found to be not only deficient but in lamentable condition; years of neglect and the Calcutta climate having taken their toll. The walls of Fort were in many places crumbling away through lack of maintenance. Much of the timberwork along the parapets was so rotten that it could not possibly support the weight of cannon. The flank wall of the Fort facing east had been broken open in several places to let light and air into the warehouses within and never properly repaired. A large warehouse had been constructed against the south flank wall in such a way as to make it impossible to provide any flanking fire from either of the two south bastions.

The condition of available munitions was, if anything, even worse. A number of the timber carriages of the cannon had rotted, rendering the guns unmanouverable and therefore useless. A whole consignment of 50 new canon and ammunition delivered three years previously, had simply been left to rust on the riverbank where the shipment had been unloaded. Within the Fort nobody had thought to ensure that the available supplies of gunpowder were stored in dry conditions, with the result that much of it was found to be damp and unusable.

There had not even, until now, been a proper assessment of the strength of the garrison. When this was hurriedly undertaken it was found that more than a third of available men were in hospital or otherwise too sick for duty. The total available strength was 180 men, of which only 45 were Europeans. In a state verging on panic, the Council hastily made plans to form a militia from the Company's civil personnel and any crew who could be spared from the Company's ships riding at anchor on the Hooghly.

As to the wider defence of the City, or at least 'White Town', no plan existed: the battle, when it came, would have to be fought from within the Fort itself. This was made more difficult by the presence of the large mansions which had been allowed to be built to the north, south and east of the Fort and which seriously restricted the field of fire. The Company's engineer had proposed blowing up these mansions; an idea vociferously rejected by the Council, concerned at the likely level of compensation the owners would demand of the Company.

The measures finally settled upon involved the digging of a defensive ditch across 'The Park' facing the Fort's eastern flank; erecting batteries at the main access points to the north south and east and palisades to block off the smaller streets. This was the first line of defence; the second and final line was the perimeter walls of the Fort itself.

By Monday 14th June, word reached the Governor that the Nawab had issued orders forbidding all native merchants and shopkeepers from supplying the Fort with provisions on pain of death. The leading columns of the Nawab's army were by then only one day's march from Calcutta. The decision was taken immediately to gather all the Europeans, their arms and provisions within the confines of the Fort to await the inevitable assault on the City.

On 16th June the Nawab's army had reached the northern and eastern outskirts of Calcutta. The first armed assault occurred that day on Perrin's Redoubt, a small fortification just to the north of Bagbazar. Why the Nawab's commanders chose to attack this, the only defended position along the whole length of the Maratha Ditch, is a mystery to which no satisfactory answer has ever been forthcoming. The assault was unsuccessful, the Nawab's troops suffering considerable casualties in the repeated attacks they made. The next day Calcutta was in flames.

What came to be later known as the Great Fire of Calcutta was the result of the predations of the hordes of plunderers sent by the Nawab into 'Black Town', to the north east of the Fort. The fires began in the Great Bazar, around current day Bagbazar, and spread rapidly southwards, encompassing the whole of the native quarter, almost to the northern perimeters of the Fort itself, a distance of nearly three and a half kilometres. The inferno raged all night and well into the next day sending hordes of the terrified and displaced inhabitants fleeing for safety into the perimeters of the Fort. By daybreak on the 18th June, more than two thousand native women and children had stormed into the Fort.

With smoke still hanging over the City, the main force of the Nawab's army had massed at the easternmost end of 'The Avenue', round about where today's Sealdah Railway Station is located. Advancing westwards along 'The Avenue' the Nawab's troops met their first resistance at the point then known as 'The Cross Roads', approximating to today's Rabindra Sarani crossing. Detachments of defenders from the Fort had manned an old jail at this location, pouring fire on the approaching enemy. West of 'The Cross Roads' lay the mansions of Rope Walk and the main eastern battery. Fierce fighting continued throughout the morning, ceasing around noon then resuming when the sun sank lower in the afternoon. The advance defenders fell back from the old jail, which had been all but destroyed in the fighting, to the empty mansions of Rope Walk. House to house fighting continued throughout the afternoon with one mansion after another being taken by the attackers then retaken by the defenders. The eastern battery proved, initially, to be a formidable advance defence with its eighteen pounder canon wreaking devastation on the Nawab's advancing troops and whichever of the surrounding buildings they had captured and occupied. As the day wore on the exhausted defenders knew that they faced an impossible task given the overwhelming odds stacked against them. As dusk fell, the defenders withdrew to the Fort abandoning the forward defences to the Nawab's troops. The Fort was now, effectively besieged.

Within the Fort conditions were chaotic; the entire parade ground taken over by the multitude which had fled the sacking of 'Black Town'. The insufficiency of supplies of clean water, primitive sanitary conditions and threat of disease, combined to make intolerable any prospect of a long siege. It was decided that the European women and children be evacuated to the Company's ships anchored in the river immediately behind the Fort. This was to be conducted under cover of darkness and in great secrecy to avoid the almost certain stampede which would occur if the hapless refugees from 'Black Town' gained any inkling of what was occurring. During the evacuation, two members of the Council, Charles Manningham and William Frankland contrived to get themselves aboard one the ships, justifying their cowardly desertion by claiming they acting as protectors to the women and children.

As dawn rose on Saturday, the 19th June, the enemy canon opened fire from the captured east battery, repeatedly pounding the Fort's eastern flank wall. Fierce fighting continued in the few remaining outposts still held by the Europeans, most particularly in Company House, south of the Fort and Mr Cruttenden's mansion to the north which, together, controlled access to the river frontage. The Nawab's commanders were well aware of the strategic importance of these two buildings which, if they could be captured, would allow their troops to encircle the Fort. Company House was the first to succumb under constant attack throughout the morning; Cruttenden's mansion was to follow some hours later, the defenders withdrawing into the Fort.

The fighting now was at its most intense with fire arrows hissing down into the Fort and skirmishing taking place right against the perimeter walls. Within the Fort, chaos reigned; the terrified refugees from 'Black Town' driven to panic, stampeded for the river, in the process further weakening the already precarious defences. Amidst all this confusion, first the garrison commander, Captain Commandant Minchin then Governor Drake deserted the Fort; the remaining defenders witnessing from the ramparts their flight to the Company ship 'Dodaldy' anchored in the Hooghly.

There now remained in the Fort fewer than 200 of the original defenders and faced with such overwhelming odds it was now only a matter of time before the Fort fell. The defenders were nevertheless to hold out until the following day, Sunday, 20th June. By then, left with hardly any usable dry gunpowder for the canon, the Senior Magistrate, John Zephaniah Holwell who had assumed command of the Fort, sent word to the Nawab seeking a truce. By four that afternoon the Nawab's troops had entered the Fort.

The immediate aftermath of the capture of the Fort is described in Footnote 2. Longer term, Calcutta (or 'Alinagar' as the Nawab had renamed the City), was recaptured in January of the following year by a force jointly led by Robert Clive and Admiral Charles Watson. The subsequent Battle of Plassey in the following June firmly established the rule of the East India Company in Bengal and saw the replacement of Siraj ud-Daulah by Mir Jafar as Nawab.

Footnote 2 - The Black Hole of Calcutta:

There was a time, within comparatively recent memory, when every British schoolboy and schoolgirl knew, or thought they knew, the story of the 'Black Hole of Calcutta'. Indeed it had long ago been embraced within the English language as a term of popular description for any crowded or tightly packed space. The factual background to this historic event however, is more elusive and controversial.

Following the fall of Calcutta and the capture of the old Fort William on 20th June, 1756 (described in Footnote 1), the surviving rear guard defenders under the command of the Magistrate, John Zephaniah Holwell together with a number of civilians still left in the Fort, were taken prisoner by soldiers of the Nawab of Bengal, Siraj-ud-Daula.

Holwell was the most senior of the East India Company's servants left in the Fort, the others, including the Governor and the Garrison Commander having escaped (some would say of these two, deserted), by river. He was brought before the Nawab and questioned as to the whereabouts of the treasure the Nawab had expected would be found in the Fort. Holwell had no knowledge of this and although disbelieved, he did eventually, secure from the Nawab an assurance that he and the other prisoners would be properly treated.

At first all seemed well. Holwell and the other prisoners were placed under very light guard in an area of the parade ground between the east gate and the Governor's house, which, together with other areas of the Fort, had by now been set ablaze on the orders of the Nawab. The intention had been that the prisoners would be held overnight in the open fronted barracks facing the parade ground between the Fort's east gate and south east bastion.

Just after sunset, events took a sudden and dramatic turn for the worse which was to have tragic consequences. It seems from accounts that an argument broke out between one of the prisoners, an apparently drunken Dutch mercenary, and one of the Nawab's soldiers resulting in the discharge of a musket causing the death of the latter.

Fearing that it would be dangerous to continue to leave the body of prisoners relatively at large throughout the night, the Nawab's troop commander, Roy Doolub urgently consulted the Nawab recommending that the prisoners be confined securely. The Nawab ordered that the prisoners be confined wherever it had been customary for the Europeans to confine their own miscreants. This was the prison cell near the Fort's south east bastion commonly referred to as the 'Black Hole'. It was as simple as that. The tragedy which was to follow was not, as some legend has it, a calculated act of vengeful barbarity. It is highly unlikely that the Nawab had ever seen the 'Black Hole' or had any idea of whether it was suitable to house such a body of prisoners. This is borne out in the testimony given by survivors to the East India Company's subsequent inquiry into the fall of the Fort. The same cannot so easily be said for the Nawab's senior officers, including his commander, Roy Doolub who had only that day inspected the 'Black Hole'. There can be little doubt that they were, or should have been fully aware of the likely consequences of confining so many prisoners in a cell with a floor space measuring slightly less than 24 square metres, ventilated only by two small, barred window openings and, moreover, in the hottest and most humid season of the year. So too would have been Holwell and a few of the soldier prisoners who were familiar with the 'Black Hole', the remainder would have had no inkling of the horror to come.

The prisoners were immediately and unceremoniously forced through the door into the 'Black Hole' cell some being trampled immediately under the torrent of bodies pushed in behind them. By the time the cell door was forced shut, 145 souls, including 12 wounded officers and one civilian woman had been thrust and crammed inside. The time was around 8 pm on the evening of Sunday 20th June.

The cell was not opened again until dawn on the following day by which time 123 of the prisoners had died from heat stroke, dehydration crushing or suffocation. Holwell was among the 22 to survive that hellish night.

Holwell's personal account of that night in the 'Black Hole' is contained in a letter written on his voyage back home to England some nine months after the event. That letter to 'a friend in whom the greatest confidence was placed' was never intended for publication and reveals far more of the personal passion and emotion evoked by that terrible night than the more sober, impersonal and almost clinical official account of the siege and downfall of the Fort which he prepared for the East India Company's subsequent inquiry into events.

There is still considerable controversy surrounding the story of the 'Black Hole'. There are those, among them some quite eminent historians, who dispute the number of victims, claiming a far lower death toll of anything between 43 and 60. A few go so far as to maintain that the event was a complete fiction, made up and promoted by the British to excuse the dominion over India which followed as a direct result of the fall of Calcutta. Where, on balance, does the truth lie?

So far as the true number of victims is concerned, those who claim a lesser number than in Holwell's account base their argument upon a reference to only 43 of the Fort's garrison being listed as missing after the event and claim, in consequence, that this must be the maximum number who died in the 'Black Hole'. Holwell's account however, is quite clear in stating that not all the prisoners, for example the civilians, European mercenaries, and 'Portuguese' (by which was generally meant Anglo-Indians), would have been listed as members of the garrison. Then there is the argument that it would have been impossible for as many adult people as Holwell claimed to have been physically contained within an area of the dimensions of the 'Black Hole'. There was even an exercise undertaken to try to prove this. A Bengali landlord, one Bholanath Chunder, fenced off an area of 24 square metres and counted the number of his tenants who could be crammed into it. This was claimed to be less than the 145 of Holwell's account. However, theoretically, each of the 145 people of Holwell's account would have had a maximum of a little over half a square metre of floor area. This is not greatly below the 0.9 square metre per person standard for modern subway travel (which in rush hours is often exceeded). Moreover, subway densities are designed to ensure that passengers do not perish.

The numbers who perished in the 'Black Hole' will probably never definitively be established. So far as is known, no head count was made of those taken prisoner when the Fort fell and since they were left only lightly guarded, it is likely that some escaped before those remaining were incarcerated in the 'Black Hole'. But does it really matter? Whether the true figure is 43 or 60 or 123 or something else altogether, what happended was still an avoidable tragedy.

There is also the claim that there is no corroboration of Holwell's account of the 'Black Hole'; that no other source mentions the incident. This is not the case. The standard three-volume reference work on this period of British History, (Bengal in 1756-57 by C.R. Hill), contains more than a thousand pages of documentary evidence and verbatim testimony by survivors of the incident. Holwell's account of events was also confirmed in all essential detail by two other survivors, Captain Mills of the garrison who kept a small diary of the event and John Cooke, the Secretary to the Governor, in his evidence under oath at the subsequent committee of inquiry.

As for the claims that the event itself never happened, this seems unlikely. Given the seemingly irrefutable evidence to the contrary, one suspects that the adoption of such a position can only be motivated by reasons other than a search for historical accuracy.

Footnote 3 - The Sino-Indian Conflict, 1962:

The relevance of the conflict, in the context of this work, is the resultant effect the hostilities had upon Calcutta's long established population of Chinese descent.

The causes of the conflict centred on a long standing dispute between India and China over sovereignty of two remote, mountainous, sparsely populated and widely separated border areas; the Aksai Chin region in the north west of the sub continent and Arunachal Pradesh (part of the old North East Frontier Agency region) in the extreme north east. The Aksai Chin region was claimed by India as belonging to Kashmir and by China as part of that country's Xinjiang province. Arunachel Pradesh, bordering Tibet, was similarly claimed by both nations. The official boundaries had been set down in the 19th century by what became known as the Johnson line covering the Akasi Chin region and the McMahon line covering the extreme north east, including Arunachal Pradesh. The complexities and inaccuracies of these boundaries are far beyond the scope of this note. Suffice to say that, at the outbreak of hostilities in 1962, Aksai Chin was occupied by China and Arunachal Pradesh by India.

So far as China was concerned, their claim over both these areas took on a new significance following that country's invasion of Tibet in 1950 and the continuing fears that India was seeking to destabilise China's control by perceived interference in Tibet's internal affairs. This was significantly heightened in 1959 when India granted asylum to the Dalai Lama who had fled Lhasa after a failed Tibetan uprising against Chinese rule.

India viewed with equal concern the placing of Chinese border posts within the disputed area of Aksai Chin and

China's construction of a highway infringing Indian claimed territory, south of the Johnson line, linking Xingjiang province with Tibet.

Various border conflicts and 'military incidents' in the years leading up to and throughout the first part of 1962, culminated in India moving forward mountain troops in an attempt to cut off Chinese lines of supply. A larger build up of Chinese forces all along the shared border and the stage was set for war. On 20th October 1962, China launched two attacks, almost 1,000 kilometres apart, in the Aksai Chin region and another along the Namka Chu River in Arunachal Pradesh.

The war is notable for the very harsh conditions under which much of the fighting took place, entailing combat in freezing conditions and at altitudes above 4,000 metres. In these conditions, both sides suffered very heavy casualties.

By the middle of November and following a number of military setbacks by India, China had advanced and secured a line of control over the area it claimed in Aksai Chin. China then halted its advance and of 19th November, declared a unilateral ceasefire.

India's Nehru administration faced harsh criticism from within for failing to anticipate and to plan properly for the Chinese invasion. The obvious unpreparedness of the Indian Army created particular anger and resulted in the resignation of the Defence Minister, Khrishna Menon.

Within India, the aftermath of the war saw a huge surge in patriotism and a corresponding increase in anti Chinese feeling and suspicion of the long established indigenous Chinese communities such as that of Calcutta. For such communities it was the beginning of the end. Many had been interned by the Indian authorities as a result of the outbreak of hostilities, others who had not been, were witness to ugly scenes as mobs attacked and burned Chinese businesses and homes. For these communities, their prospects were grim; there seemed little future for them within India. In Calcutta, as within other Indian cities, there began a wholesale break up of Chinese communities, huge numbers migrating abroad, to the United States, Canada, Australia and Europe. Today, in what was once the thronged China Town of central Calcutta, few Chinese remain. Those that do, mainly the elderly, are the last of the line.

The border disputes remain essentially unresolved to this day.

Footnote 4 - *The Calcutta Riots of 1946*:

Few who know the place would dispute the underlying volatility of Calcutta or its capacity to erupt into civil disturbance and violence with alarming ease and rapidity.

The reasons for this are complex and are seemingly woven into the political and social fabric of the City. It cannot be explained in terms of a straightforward preponderance of Calcuttans to law breaking since, of all the larger conurbations of the sub-continent, Calcutta actually has the lowest recorded crime rate at 71 offences per 100,000 head of population. This is less than half the national rate recorded in the 2006 Report of the (Indian) National Crime Records Bureau, of 167 per 100,000 and is far lower than the comparative recorded figures for London, Paris or Rome.

The answer, if there is one, is more likely to be found in the historical traditions of Bengali politics and the complexities of Calcutta's ethnic mix which is representative of almost every corner of the sub-continent and beyond. It has even been suggested that the low female to male ratio of the City's populace (828 females to 1,000 males) accounted for by the large numbers of migrant single male workers, may have something to do with it.

Whatever the reasons, civil disturbance, riot and curfew are not infrequent features of life in Calcutta. I cannot remember any visit I have made to the City without some such incident being reported. These outbreaks of disorder are often triggered by some seemingly mundane occurrence such as a traffic fatality, some overzealous police action or a hike in retail prices or public transport fares.

Far worse have been the communal riots between Calcutta's Hindus, Muslims and other religious groups, made more sinister wherever the conflict appears to have been engineered or purposely stoked. There had been serious communal riots in 1918, and 1926 and sporadic but less serious outbreaks throughout the 1930's. A common feature with nearly all of these outbreaks was the speed with which inflammatory leaflets appeared on the streets immediately violence had erupted, suggesting a degree of planning.

Bad as these events may have been, they were as nothing compared to the maelstrom of violence which enveloped Calcutta in 1946 when the City, gripped in a murderous frenzy, sought to destroy itself.

The lead up to the great riots of 1946 coincided with and was inextricably linked to the impasse which had by then been reached between the Indian National Congress and the Muslim League, the two largest parties in the Constituent Assembly of India. In an attempt to move forward the transfer of power from the British Raj to Indian leadership in the face of opposition from the Muslim League led by Muhammad Ali Jinnah, a proposal had been made to divide the British Raj between a Hindu majority India and a Muslim majority Pakistan. The nominally independent Princely States were to be allowed to choose which of the two new nations they wished to join or to remain independent. This compromise proposal was rejected outright by the Indian National Congress led by Jawaharlal Nehru. This led to the Muslim League boycotting the Constituent Assembly amidst dark mutterings from Jinnah that if the Muslims were not granted a Pakistan then the League would launch 'Direct Action' to force the issue. This was followed up in the last week of July 1946, with the announcement by Jinnah that Friday 16th August, 1946 would be 'Direct Action Day'. This was delivered with a warning to the Indian National Congress that 'we do not want war, if you want war we accept your offer unhesitatingly. We shall have India divided or we shall have India destroyed'.

Muslims throughout India were called upon by Jinnah to observe 'Direct Action Day' on which, in support of the League's demands, meetings and processions would be held throughout the country, widespread strikes held and the business of Government disrupted. By and large, throughout the country this passed off with only limited civil disturbances. There was one dreadful and hellish exception - Calcutta.

In Calcutta, from the start of the year, there had been strike after strike interspersed with sporadic but limited outbreaks of communal violence. Thanks to a series of inflammatory speeches by both League and Congress politicians in the State Assembly, communal tensions were already running high when Huseyn Shaheed Suhrawardy, the Chief Minister of Bengal and leader of the Muslim League administration in the Bengal State Assembly, made the fatal declaration that 16th August, the date of 'Direct Action Day', would be a public holiday in the State. In declaring this public holiday the intention may simply have been to ensure the highest possible turnout of League sympathisers at the mass rally, which would convene at the foot of the Ochterlony Monument on the afternoon of Direct Action Day. However, the clear danger, foreseen by many, was that the public holiday would also ensure that more League supporters would be on the streets to enforce strikes in Hindu areas of the City and that more Congress supporters would be there to resist them. Whatever the real reasons for declaring a public holiday to coincide with 'Direct Action Day', the consequences were to prove deadly.

Friday 16th August, a hot and humid day, began quite normally. Buses and taxis were running but not the trams; the drivers, fearing trouble, having called a one day strike. At about 7.30 am reports were coming in to police headquarters in Lal Bazar that Hindus had barricaded the Tala and Belgachia Bridges to prevent Muslim processions from entering the City and linking up with others en route to the Ochterlony Monument.

Throughout the rest of the Friday morning, the police were receiving reports of houses and shops being looted and set alight in the north and east of the City and of random assaults and stabbings. The violence was clearly communal in nature and was to remain so throughout the hell which was to follow.

By 2.00 pm, with various Muslim processions converging on the Ochterlony Monument reports were coming in that at Sealdah and Bow Bazar, the police had opened fire and used tear gas to disperse violent mobs bent on communal strife. Military units were placed on standby to move out to the main trouble spots should the situation deteriorate further; the plan being that they would secure and keep open the main roads throughout the City, freeing up police for other work.

A little over an hour later, Mr Suhrawardy began addressing the massive crowd of League supporters, variously estimated at around 100,000, which had gathered at the foot of the Ochterlony Monument. As if the situation was not already bad enough, Mr Suhrawardy announced that, after visiting Muslim areas in the City and having found the inhabitants peaceful, he had arranged with police and military that 'they would not interfere'. Neither the police nor the military had given any such undertaking and whatever Mr Suhrawardy had meant to convey by his announcement, many in the massive crowd before him took it as an open invitation to riot.

As soon as the crowd began to disperse, reports flooded in of further looting and burning of Hindu shops and homes in the central areas of the City. Lorries full of Muslim men armed with clubs, spears and bottles were seen driving up and down Chitteranjan Avenue and Mahatma Ghandi Road. In the trouble spots fierce retaliatory attacks were being made by gangs of armed Hindus and Sikhs, adding further to the carnage. Mobile patrols of troops were sent out to sweep and gain intelligence on the neighbourhoods closest to the main thoroughfares although little was still known about the situation in the bustees.

By 6.00 pm a curfew had been imposed on all the worst affected districts of the City. A few hours later a mobile troop patrol en route to Howrah to quell serious disturbances, found most of College Street ablaze; the few still unburned shops and houses having been sacked, their contents littering the roadway. Further looting and arson was taking place along the upper reaches of the Circular Road around Sealdah and in Mahatma Ghandi Road. As yet there was no outward evidence of the terrible killings which had taken place; the streets were clear of bodies.

By daybreak on Saturday 17th, dead bodies began to appear on the streets and the furious killings started afresh. Police and military patrols reported that often they would pass along a road and all was clear, only to return ten minutes later to find several bodies, sometimes in the roadway, sometimes in the entrances of buildings or heaped onto trucks. The lanes and gullees of central and north Calcutta provided both points of ambush and routes of escape for the armed groups in their murderous work. They would emerge from these byways, stab or bludgeon their victims to death and melt away by the same route only to re-emerge elsewhere to continue their savagery.

Mid morning saw numerous fires along Mahatma Ghandi Road and the gathering of large angry mobs of armed men. Every time these were scattered by police and troops using baton charges and tear gas, they would melt away into the surrounding lanes only to re-emerge and reform the minute the patrols had passed, leaving the bodies of their latest victims in their wake.

The afternoon saw rioting spread to some of the southern parts of the City with the same kind of fury seen in the northern and central districts where bodies continued to pile up on the streets. Reports were coming in of heavy fighting around Park Circus, along Dharmatala Street and as far afield as Garden Reach, Kiddepore and Beliagatia. A pall of smoke hung over the City from the many buildings torched by the rioters. By nightfall tanks equipped with searchlights had been deployed in the most troubled districts, their powerful lights flickering over the devastation and the dead as they rumbled from street to street on their patrols.

In the early hours of Sunday, the 18th, the military moved Gurkha troops into the docks area at Kiddepore. In the central and northern districts of the City, the military increased its presence on the streets, posting static guard units at main junctions and other strategic points and sending out mobile patrols to sweep adjacent areas. Elsewhere, in the neighbourhoods not yet under control, the situation worsened almost hourly. Hijacked buses and taxis were seen all over north Calcutta, loaded with Hindus and Sikhs armed with swords, knives, iron bars and firearms. By the afternoon, Tarachand Dutta Street, Syed Sally Lane. Raj Mohan Street and the adjoining thoroughfares east of the Nakhoda Mosque were howling in riot. Military patrols were rushed into the area and opened fire with both tear gas and live rounds to clear the streets. The military command, by this time had decided to reinforce Calcutta with further Divisions being ordered from Ranchi, and Ramgarh.

At about the same time, a column headed by two light tanks on the way to relieve troops in the military dominated areas, was diverted to the Jorabagan and Shyambazar neighbourhoods of north Calcutta where serious rioting was reported. Heading north up what is now called Rabindra Sarani and once past the Vivekananda Road crossing, the column found the roadways strewn with the contents of sacked houses and shops, some of which were already on fire. The devastation grew worse the further north the column moved so that at the Grey Street crossing (present day Sri Arabinda Sarani junction), the column had to halt to clear away the scores of bodies littering their path, before dealing with a frenzied mob which had gathered a few hundred metres further on at the junction of Shyambazar Street. Here the roadway was littered with more than 120 corpses with scores more found in the surrounding side streets.

The further the column probed the more bodies it found. At the Shobabazar Market and in the surrounding bustees, a wholesale slaughter had taken place with bodies strewn about everywhere. In some of the adjoining shanties the bodies of whole families were discovered, murdered before they could flee. Other parts of the bustees had been burned to the ground, the fate of the inhabitants unknown.

By dusk on the Sunday the military had finally gained complete control of all of the trouble spots of central and north Calcutta; the worst was over, it was as if the City lay exhausted, temporarily sated by the murderous fury of the preceding days.

It is unlikely that the actual numbers of dead and injured will ever be determined to any degree of accuracy. Bodies were still being found weeks later, retrieved from the sewers, tanks and ditches into which they had been unceremoniously pitched or discovered amongst the charred wreckage of what had once been homes and shops. It has been estimated that more than 150,000 people fled the City ahead of the worst of the violence and that a further 100,000 were made homeless as a result of the destruction wreaked. The numbers of dead have been put at anything between 4,000 and 7,000 and the injured at up to 100,000.

The aftermath of the great riots left Calcutta's infrastructure is a state of disintegration and saw the threat of epidemics, food shortages and hyperinflation as commodity prices escalated. Sporadic and isolated incidents of communal violence in the City continued throughout the remainder of 1946.

There would be other serious riots in Calcutta, notably throughout much of the 1960's and 1970's but never anything on a scale or ferocity as the events of 1946.

Footnote 5 - The Bengal Famine of 1943:

Periodic famines have visited Bengal and many other parts of India probably since the dawn of time. Of those recorded for Bengal, the worst is reputed to have been the famine of 1770. This famine, together with the epidemics of disease which nearly always attend such catastrophes, is said to have killed up to one third of Bengal's population. There were six further famines, not all of which were restricted to Bengal alone, recorded between 1783 and 1897. But of all the famines to ravage Bengal, perhaps the most frequently recalled is that of 1943, not only because this is the most recent but also because there are good grounds for believing that with better planning and more efficient distribution of available food supplies it could have been avoided or at least its impact considerably lessened.

The calamitous famine which occurred in 1943 has been described, with some justification, as a man made or artificial famine in the sense that it occurred whilst there was only a minimal actual food shortage overall in Bengal and sufficient additional supplies were available from elsewhere in India.

The causes of the famine are many and complex; some relating to natural occurrences, others involving matters of official policy, failure properly to evaluate what was happening and to take timely corrective action and frankly, a degree of indifference. The British as rulers at the time must take a good share of the blame for what transpired. The popularly held view in India that all blame for the catastrophe rests solely with the British administration is understandable but overlooks the inconvenient fact that, throughout the entire period, Bengal had a State Government sitting in Calcutta comprising almost exclusively

Indian nationals. The role of Ministers of the State Government in consistently downplaying the looming calamity was a major contributory factor to the severity of the famine.

In the decade up to 1941, except for the odd year here and there, Bengal had experienced less than satisfactory harvests of the staples, rice and grain. Official records of the crops during this period had been hopelessly inadequate, providing little useful information on which to forecast future yields or the likely levels of imports required should the harvest fail.

Supplies of rice from Burma, which had been one of the major outside sources of supply to top up Bengal's indifferent harvests, were no longer available following the fall of the country to the Japanese at the beginning of 1942. The proximity of hostilities to Bengal and fears of an imminent Japanese invasion had created additional strains on supply. In this climate of uncertainty, the peasant farmers were cautious about releasing all their produce onto the markets. It is estimated that as much as one third of what was normally available to the market was held back. This coupled with pressures of demand brought about by consumers, anxious to ensure a supply of the staples, making larger than normal purchases, led to price increases and hoarding. This hoarding was hardly surprising given that at the outbreak of war, the State Government had exhorted householders to set by and keep at least two months' stock of the basics in their homes.

Fears of invasion also led to the institution of 'denial to the enemy' measures. These included the removal from Bengal's vulnerable coastal districts of any supplies of rice and paddy considered surplus to local requirements. A further measure required that every craft in the State to be registered under military supervision to prevent an important form of river and coastal transport falling into enemy hands. The effect of this was to take upwards of 20,000 small craft out of commission, seriously diminishing the ability to maintain fishing or the proper cultivation of the delta lands.

All of these factors had combined to push up the retail price of rice to such an extent that in June 1942 the State Government issued an order fixing the maximum price on the Calcutta market. The immediate effect of this was that all supplies suddenly disappeared from Calcutta and many other districts in Bengal; the suppliers being unwilling to sell within the artificially imposed price ceiling. The government's answer to this sudden scarcity was to move into Calcutta some of the stocks of surplus rice and grain removed from the coastal districts as part of the 'denial to the enemy' measures. These transferred stocks were distributed to the ration shops used by the general public and to the employers of industrial labour who had organised their own purchasing schemes for employees. At the same time, the authorities recognised the negative impact on supply on the maximum price controls and these became to be enforced only in the most flagrant cases of profiteering. Accompanied by a temporary embargo on exports of staples to other parts of India, the cumulative effect of these measures did achieve some easing of the pressures on supply and retail prices.

Soon after, disaster struck. In October 1942 a ferocious tropical cyclone struck the coastal districts of Bengal, devastating the winter paddy crop (known as the aman crop). This was closely followed by crop disease which further depleted the harvest all over Bengal.

Japanese air raids on Calcutta throughout the final weeks of December 1942, led to the closure of a large number of food grain shops. This in turn led to the State Government requisitioning existing food stocks within the City and distributing these through controlled shops and approved markets. To replace these requisitioned stocks and maintain supply the Government launched a procurement programme, prescribing maximum purchase prices. This was not successful and was quickly abandoned, leading to an increase in supply but also to massive increases in retail prices. Rice which had been selling at around six rupees per maund (about nine kilos), at the beginning of 1942 rose to over thirty rupees by May and eventually was to increase to over one hundred rupees in some districts of the State.

At around the same time, the Chief Minister of the State Government, Mr Fazlul Huq at a food conference held in Delhi announced that 'We (Bengal) do not require for the next few months, any rice, even though we are in deficit.' This level of complacency was to typify the State Governments approach to the looming catastrophe over the months to come. The State's Minister for Food, one Mr Huseyn Shaheed Suhrawardy, (the very same man who, three years later as Bengal's Chief Minister, would play such a pivotal contributory role in the murderous riots which were to engulf and nearly destroy Calcutta), declared that, although there were some difficulties due to hoarding and profiteering, there was a sufficiency of foodgrain for the people. Confidence indeed when it was already clear that the winter harvest would be very seriously depleted.

Mr Suhrawardy did at least get one thing right, there had been profiteering and on a grand scale. The subsequent Famine Inquiry Commission was to conclude that the deficiency in supply was probably only about 6% of requirement and that the increase in prices was therefore, grossly disproportionate. To make matters even worse, if that were possible, foodgrain was still being exported from Bengal to other parts of India. It has been estimated that, whilst people starved, some 80,000 tons left Bengal in the first half of 1943. It is difficult to comprehend, even at a distance of more than half a century, how such incompetence or callous indifference was possible in the face of what was by then an undeniable emergency.

In the hinterlands of Bengal people began to starve and to die, at first in isolated instances then in their scores and hundreds; whole families, whole villages. Many had already lost every-thing in the recent cyclone and floods. Others, rendered desti-tute by the winter crop failure had already sold whatever little they possessed. Where they did not die in the countryside or the delta lands, the stronger ones, driven by desperate hunger, left their villages and began roaming the land looking for food; a good many made for Calcutta.

In Calcutta, what began as a trickle of the newly arrived and starving adding to the City's already high quota of misery, quickly became a torrent. Huddled along the banks of the Circular Canal, besides the tracks of the suburban railways or lining the City's streets, the starving multitudes could no longer be ignored by an officialdom which seemingly, had until then had its head stuck firmly in the sand. Even so, it took relentless reporting by newspapers of the unfolding tragedy to shame the authorities into any sort of action. There is clear evidence that both State Government Ministers and the British administra-tion sought wherever possible to suppress, distort or play down what was happening and clear for all to see. The State Govern-ment tried to ban newspaper reporters from describing the dead as victims of starvation. Instead those dying of hunger were to be described as 'sick destitutes'. The ever less than candid, State Food Minister Suhrawardy, as late as July 1943 was resisting calls to declare Bengal a famine area on the grounds that it was 'not necessary'. In London, the Secretary of State for India was telling Parliament that the death rate in Bengal was running at about one thousand a week 'or a bit higher'. The true death rate was at least ten times that figure.

Charities had for months been operating pavement kitchens in the streets of the City. This was later to be followed by Government feeding centres both in Calcutta and elsewhere in Bengal. By the end of the year, throughout Bengal, more than two million souls would be queuing daily at these feeding centres. Belatedly in October, Bengal Food Minister Suhrawardy was to finally announce that 'Bengal is in the grip of an unprecedented famine'.

Following closely on Mr Suhrawardy's announcement, the State Government passed legislation in the form of the Bengal Destitute Persons (Repatriation and Relief) Ordinance which allowed the police to clear starving people from the streets of Calcutta and send them back from whence they had come. In the following three months more than forty thousand 'sick destitutes' were excluded from the City under these powers.

Death tolls continued to rise for now starvation had been joined by epidemics of cholera, smallpox, malaria and pneumonia cutting their swathe across Bengal. The death rate probably peaked in December following the successful winter harvest and the arrival of food supplies from other parts of India. This led to a considerable lowering of the retail price of rice and a consequent decline in the intensity of the famine. Death rates accross Bengal although reducing, were to remain higher than the pre famine levels throughout 1944 and into the first few months of 1945.

The total number of people who died as a result of the 1943 famine and its attendant epidemics of disease is still a matter of great controversy. It was certainly far less than the figure of twelve millions often quoted in Indian Communist Party literature but considerably higher than the official estimate of one and a half millions given in the official report of the Famine Inquiry Commission. In 1945, studies undertaken by academics of Calcutta University were confidently quoting a more probable estimated total death toll of around three and a half millions. Statistical argument in the face of such horrifying and incomprehensible numbers seems almost meaningless for it does nothing to alter the cataclysmic nature of what took place.

Footnote 6 - *The Nuncomar Controversy:*

The story really begins during Warren Hastings' first stint in Bengal from 1750 until 1764. Following the Battle of Plassey and the retaking of Calcutta, Hastings was appointed in 1758 to the important post of Resident at the Mughal court of Murshidabad. It was in this post, which he was to hold for three years, that he first came into conflict with Nuncomar, a Bengali Brahman and titled member of the Mughal aristocracy. Nuncomar, who had been the Governor of Hooghly and had the ear of the Nawab, Mir Jafar, appears to have been an inveterate and rascally intriguer, constantly trying to play both ends off against the middle. He was left dangerously exposed and discredited when in 1760 the Nawab was deposed and replaced by his son-in-law, Mir Kasim. This reputation for untrustworthiness and double dealing is almost certainly at the heart of why Hastings took such uncharacteristic dislike against Nuncomar; an enmity fully reciprocated.

In 1761, Hastings was made a member of the Council of the Presidency, under the Governorship of Henry Vansittart. At this time practically all the servants of the East India Company were traders in their private capacity and claimed, for themselves and any of their native subordinates, various privileges and exemptions from taxes and local jurisdiction. This not only placed the native princes at serious disadvantage and led to wide ranging corruption, but struck at the very authority of Mughal government. Vansittart, backed by Hastings sought, without success, to check these abuses and in so doing made powerful enemies amongst important vested interests. The situation led first to a rupture with the Nawab and then to hostilities only brought to an end in 1764 with the decisive victory of Buxar over the allied armies of Bengal and Oudh. Both Vansittart and Hastings then resigned their seats in disgust and returned to England.

Warren Hastings returned to India in late 1768 having been appointed to a seat on the Council of the Madras Presidency. By 1772, Hastings was back in Calcutta, this time as Governor General. In 1770, the worst recorded Indian famine had swept away a credibly estimated one-third of the population of Bengal and had so seriously impacted upon the finances of the East India Company that by 1772 loans were being sought from the Bank of England to prop up the Company. The loans were refused and the Company was only rescued by the intervention of the British Government with a loan of £1 million pounds. The cost of that loan was high with the Company's dividend being limited to six percent until the loan was repaid with surplus revenue being paid over to the Exchequer. More significant was the Regulating Act, passed by Parliament in 1773. This legislation effected considerable changes in the constitution of the Bengal government and required the appointment of a Royal, rather than Company, Governor General, based in Calcutta and having overall authority over the Madras and Bombay Presidencies as well. Hastings was named in the Act as this Governor General for a term of five years. The Act also established a supreme court of judicature comprising a Chief Justice and three puisne judges to exercise jurisdiction at Calcutta. The first to occupy the Chief Justice post was Sir Elijah Impey.

The whole thrust of the Regulating Act was to establish for the first time the influence of the Crown, (Parliament) in Indian affairs. Hastings was to rule the new Council with four other Members each, crucially, with a vote equal to his own: therein being the source of nearly all his immediate difficulties. The new Members, with the exception of Richard Barwell, who had been born in Calcutta and had spent all of his adult life in the Bengal Civil Service, were all novices on

India. They were Parliament's nominees and this was an age when patronage was more important than ability, or even suitability. General Clavering and the Hon. Colonel Monson were both second rate, former politicians but with powerful establishment connections in England. The fourth Member was Phillip Francis, seemingly better connected than accomplished, having been a fairly lowly clerk in the War Office.

When the Indiaman carrying these three new Members docked at Chandpal Ghat in October 1774, they were met with a 17 gun salute. Their chagrin that this was not the Royal, 21 gun salute they believed their importance merited, speaks volumes about them. Further mortification was to follow. There was neither guard of honour nor any sign of the Governor General waiting to receive them ashore.

Amongst the first actions of Hastings following his appointment, was to implement the Company's instructions to bring the entire management of revenues under direct Company control. All the offices of administration were transferred from Murshidabad to Calcutta, ruining many a native reputation in the process and bringing Hastings into renewed conflict with the wily Nuncomar. At the same time a settlement of the land revenues based on leases for five years was begun and the police and military systems were reorganised and placed on a more professional footing.

From the very outset, the three newly arrived Members of the Council set out to obstruct, delay and generally to frustrate the best efforts of Hastings; Barwell invariably siding with the embattled Governor General. Taking advantage of an ambiguous clause in their commission, these three Members, the majority on the Council, sought to review all the recent measures the Governor General had implemented. All that Hastings had done, they condemned; all that they could, they reversed.

Hastings was placed in an impossible position, being reduced to a cipher at meetings of the Council.

Nuncomar, having sensed the ongoing feud within the Council and seeking to ingratiate himself with the trio of dissidents, lost no time in privately relaying to them anything he thought would be to the detriment of the Governor General. He found a ready and credible audience when he passed on to these three Members detailed allegations of Hastings' corruption in the acceptance of bribes. To charges from such a source and brought in such a manner and on such a flimsy basis, Hastings disdained to respond instead, advising his accusers to make a formal case to the Supreme Court. Undeterred, the three Member majority on the Council resolved formally that the Governor General had been guilty of peculation and ordered that he repay the bribes he had allegedly received. A few days later, Nuncomar was unceremoniously thrown into jail.

Prior to the accusation levelled against him, Hastings had, independently, been preparing papers for the Supreme Court alleging conspiracy by Nuncomar. Nuncomar's incarceration was not, however, as a result of this charge but on an entirely different charge of forgery of a bond six years previously, brought by a private prosecutor unconnected with Hastings or any of the Council Members. This apparently coincidental occurrence is the first element of the controversy which followed. The second element was the speed in which Nuncomar's trial was conducted and the sentence passed upon him carried out.

The trial, before the Chief Justice Sir Elijah Impey and the three puisne Judges of the Supreme Court took eight days from start to finish; the Court sitting, unusually, throughout the entire day as well as on a Sunday. The summing up to an all European jury was to earn Impey an impeachment hearing before the British Parliament many years later, in which he was exonerated. The hapless serial intriguer, Nuncomar was found guilty, refused leave to appeal and sentenced to be hanged as a felon. His confederates on the Council deserted him, Clavering refusing to sign a plea for clemency drafted by Francis. The sentence was carried out within seven weeks, on 5th August, 1775, ironically at a site in the area later to become known as Hastings, near to the site of the present day Vidyasagar Setu.

Many, including Thomas Macaulay, the historian and former politician, believed that Hastings had conspired with Impey to commit a judicial murder. Hastings always maintained that he did not cause the charge on which Nuncomar was convicted to be instituted. Impey's role as presiding Judge has been exhaustively examined and no real evidence found to suggest that Nuncomar did not receive a fair trial. The severity of the sentence, the denial of an appeal and the exclusively European composition of the jury are more disquieting factors.

The Nuncomer incident was but one of the many charges included in Hastings' subsequent impeachment for 'high crimes and misdemeanours' commenced in the British Parliament in 1788. Finally, in 1795 he was found innocent of all charges but despite his many, very real achievement, his Governor Generalship will always be tainted and overshadowed by the Nuncomer controversy.

Footnote 7 – War and the Birth of Bangladesh, 1971:

The war, which erupted in 1971 between what was once known as West and East Pakistan and which, subsequently, India entered, resulted in the establishment of the independent nation of Bangladesh. The relevance of the conflict in the context of this work is the massive displacement of population it caused from the area then forming East Pakistan. Millions of refugees fleeing the fighting and the violent repression that preceded it, poured across the border into India. Calcutta in particular, the nearest city of any size to the eastern border area and little more than 60 kilometres distant, saw an estimated 2 million refugees flooding into the City and its surrounding areas during this time; perhaps up to half that number taking up residence. I was witness to this tidal wave of misery and despair; it was my first experience of Calcutta and I have never forgotten it.

The partition of India in 1947 created a new state of Pakistan whose boundaries had been drawn to encompass the majority Muslim areas of British India and the various Princely States. This resulted in a single state comprising two widely separated geographical areas, one occupying the far western side of the sub-continent being originally called West Pakistan and the other, occupying the far eastern side, East Pakistan (the present day Bangladesh).

From the outset, the two halves of Pakistan were never really equal partners; West Pakistan being the politically dominant was perceived to exploit East Pakistan economically. Apart from these inescapable inequalities, there were significant cultural differences, perhaps the most controversial being that of language. In 1948, Jinnah, (Pakistan's first Governor General), had declared that the sole official national language would be Urdu, sweeping aside protestations that Bengali was the language spoken by the majority in the more populous eastern half of the country. This controversy was to lead, in the 1950's, to widespread unrest in East Pakistan which was ruthlessly suppressed, resulting in the deaths of a number of students.

Although East Pakistan accounted for a majority of the nation's population, political power remained firmly in the hands of West Pakistan and particularly, the Punjabis. As political power began to be concentrated in the President of Pakistan and later the military, Prime Ministers, the elected Chief Executives of State, became increasingly likely to be sacked at the behest of the West Pakistan political establishment, acting through the President. This was more likely to happen where the elected Prime Minister was from East Pakistan as was witnessed by the swift dismissal of Prime Ministers Nazimuddin, Ali Bogra, and Suhrawardy. The military dictatorships of Ayub Khan and Yahya Khan, both West Pakistanis, between 1958 and 1971 only added to the feeling of political impotence in East Pakistan.

Political tensions between East and West Pakistan reached crisis point when the largest of East Pakistan's political parties, the Awami League, led by Sheikh Mujibar Rahman won a landslide victory in the national elections of 1970. The League, having won a majority of the 313 seats in the National Assembly, was fully entitled under the constitution to form a government. However, the (West) Pakistan People's Party led by Zulfikar Ali Bhutto refused to accept Rahman as Prime Minister and instead proposed the country having two 'Prime Ministers', one for the West half of the country and another for the East. This, understandably, caused outrage amongst the populace in the eastern half of the country where antipathy to the political dominance of West Pakistan had already been running dangerously high.

If any further provocation was needed, this was provided by the Government's perceived handling of the aftermath of the catastrophic Bhola cyclone which struck the coastline of East Pakistan on the night of 12th November 1970. The cyclone, which made landfall at the same time as one of the highest tides of the year, was one of the deadliest ever recorded. The consequences were devastating, resulting in an estimated 500,000 dead and millions more left without food, clean water or shelter. The Government's handling of the relief efforts was lamentable. Slow to respond, failing to grasp the enormous magnitude of the disaster, the Government was seen by the eastern populace as callously indifferent to their suffering. Rallies and demonstrations were held in Dhaka calling for the resignation of the country's President. A general strike was held and a boycott placed on government work, exacerbating the already faltering and inadequate relief efforts.

By early March 1971, the Government had imposed martial law in the eastern half of the country and began deporting all foreign journalists from the region. That having been achieved, on 25th March, the Pakistani Army launched 'Operation Searchlight', designed to crush the Bengali nationalist movement once and for all. The Army quickly took control of all the major cities then began a systematic elimination of all opposition, military, political and civil. The widespread killings and other atrocities by the Pakistani Army which followed have since been well documented and, for the most part, fully substantiated. Apart from enraging the Bengalis even further and increasing their resistance, this unrestrained violence ended all the efforts which had been underway to negotiate a settlement. East Pakistan made a formal declaration of independence on 26th March and formed a government in exile. Thus began what Bangladeshis would later come to call their liberation war.

Resistance to the Pakistan Army took the form of well organised guerrilla warfare by the underground 'Mukti Bahini', bolstered by increasing numbers of defecting Bengali soldiers. The 'Mukti Bahini' was particularly successful in the border areas where they operated their training camps with material assistance from India. Every success by the 'Mukti Bahini' was met with savage reprisals by the Pakistani Army and the various Islamist militias they had set up to assist them; Hindu Bengalis often bearing the brunt of such reprisals.

At the beginning of December 1971, the Pakistan Government, wary of the level of involvement by India in support of the 'Mukti Bahini', launched a pre-emptive but largely unsuccessful air strike against Indian positions. This ultimately disastrous decision marked the beginning of the end for Pakistan in the eastern region. Pakistan's action was widely viewed as an act of unprovoked aggression against India. Indian Prime Minister Indira Gandhi declared war on Pakistan that same day and ordered the immediate mobilisation of Indian troops. This was swiftly followed by a full scale invasion across the eastern border with Indian troops being supported by the 'Mukti Bahani'. In little under a fortnight, the Indian Army had captured all major centres of population, including Dhaka. The Indian Air Force had established near total air supremacy and all major seaports had been blockaded, effectively cutting off all escape routes for the Pakistan Army. On 16th December Pakistan signed an instrument of surrender, heralding the birth of Bangladesh as an independent sovereign state.

The cumulative effect of the Bhola cyclone and the murderous outrages of the Pakistan Army in 'Operation Searchlight' which followed created one of the largest displacements of civilians ever seen. Anything up to three millions had been killed (the actual numbers will probably never be known) and a further eight to ten millions (an estimated 75% of whom were Hindus) had fled the holocaust seeking safety across India's eastern border. Prime Minister Indira Ghandi had rightly called it 'the biggest and cruellest migration in all history'

All along India's eastern border areas, from the towns of Balurghat in the north to Madhabkati in the south, a human tragedy of biblical proportions was unfolding. Thousands crossed the border daily; a seemingly endless tide of ragged, muddied, and numbed refugees trudging into India, bent low under the bundles containing all that they now possessed. At the border town of Bangaon, little more than 60 kilometres from the northern suburbs of Calcutta, the rickety makeshift shelters of the refugees stretched as far as the eye could see; covering fields still waterlogged from recent rains, lining the sides of roads, occupying every conceivable space, save anywhere near the ditches which oozed the smell of death from the corpses of those who having made that terrible journey, could continue no further.

Here and elsewhere along the border, long lines of bedraggled and empty eyed new arrivals queued, sometimes for days, to register at the reception centres set up by the Indian authorities to cope with this unprecedented and seemingly unmanageable catastrophe. Registration facilitated the compulsory inoculations which in turn allowed the issue of a ration card for just less than half a kilo of rice and a quarter kilo of pulses. The hungry multitudes queued with the patience possessed only by the completely exhausted and wholly dependent.

In Calcutta itself, those who had already penetrated the city limits could be found camped out along the platforms of Howrah and Sealdah stations, along the banks of the Circular Canal, and beside the railway tracks running from Dum Dum in the north, southwards to beyond Park Circus. As the numbers of refugees swelled, ramshackle encampments sprang up in the eastern wastelands where Salt Lake City now stands, out towards Tangra, Gobra and as far as the dumping grounds at Dhapa. Initially, lacking even the most basic amenities, these encampments were terrible and desolate places; the only consolation for the inhabitants being that here, at least, no one was trying systematically to slaughter them.

Smaller pockets of refugees were to be found almost anywhere throughout the City competing for space and compassion with the indigenous pavement dwellers and supplicants for alms. I remember particularly one small encampment of refugees out on what was once called the Lower Circular Road. Located just south of the Moulali Crossing, the encampment had spread along the pavement in front of the old Methodist Church, using the handsome Church railings as support for the crude lean-to structures they inhabited. Surmounted on top of these railings was a huge hoarding with 'Calcutta – Jesus Loves You' emblazoned on it in bold lettering; a poignant backdrop indeed.

Calcutta was ill equipped to deal with a human catastrophe on this scale landing on its doorstep. Indeed, what city would not face difficulties in such circumstances? Slowly, the authorities got to grips with the monumental problem; disused jute mills and godowns were brought into use as temporary shelter for the refugees, even in one case a redundant film studio. The central government in Delhi was committed to helping the refugees and underwrote small cash payments to help individuals rehabilitate themselves. In time, the City authorities established purpose built refugee colonies at various locations in Calcutta's outer suburbs, which are still in existence. Some of the refugees accepted government grants to relocate to the Andaman and Nicobar Islands which India was then seeking to populate and develop.

Annexe 2

Glossary

Aakh wallah	sugar cane grinder
Agarbatti	incense sticks
Aloo	potato
Anglo-Indian	Indian of mixed blood
Angrezi	English
Ashram	place of religious retreat
Auto-rickshaw	3 wheeled two stroke motorised taxi
Babu	clerk or bureaucrat
Bagh	garden
Baniya	shopkeeper or trader
Baapu	Mahatma Ghandi (lit. 'father')
Beedie	thin hand rolled poor man's cigarette
Bhaji	fried vegetables
Bheestie	traditional water carrier
Bisleri	bottled water
Burra	big or senior
Bustee	slum
Chabbi wallah	key maker
Chai	tea
Chaikhana	tea stall
Chapatti	thin Indian flatbread
Chappals	sandals
Charpoy	rope sprung bed
Charpresi	messenger
Chawl	tenement slum (more west India)
Chowk	market
Chowkidar	watchman or gatekeeper
Chota	small or junior
Countrymade	Illegally made (e.g. liquor, firearm etc)
Chula	cooking stove, wood or dung fuelled

Dal	dish of lentils or other pulses
Dalits	lowest castes (lit. the oppressed)
Darwan	gatekeeper
Devi	goddess
Dhobi	laundry
Dhoti	traditional Hindu men's loincloth
Doms	members of the caste who handle dead bodies
Dosa	plain or spicy rice flower pancake
Dupatta	scarf worn with salwar kameez
Durga	Hindu deity representing benevolent side of power
Eve	woman or women
Eve teasing	sexual harassment of females
Firang	foreign
Firinghee	foreigner
Ful jharu wallah	long cleaning stick seller
Ghat	steps to bathing or landing place on river
Ghee	clarified butter widely used in cooking
Godown	warehouse
Goonda	thug, criminal lout
Gunny	sack
Gupshup	to gossip
Harijan	untouchable castes (lit. children of God)
Havaldar	police rank between constable/ inspector
Hijra	member of a group of eunuchs
Holi	Hindu, Spring festival of colours
Idly (Idli)	rice flower dumpling, breakfast dish 'usually served with sambhar
Jaggery	unrefined coarse sugar
Jawan	soldier
Ji	respectful suffix to name, e.g. Ghandiji
Kali	Hindu deity representing the darker side of power
Kangali	person in great want
Karma	fate or destiny
Katra	sub division of a market
Khadi	hand woven cloth

Kothi	same as Katra above
Kshatriya	warrior caste
Kumar	potter caste
Kurta	man's long loose shirt
Kutcha	rough, crude, unsophisticated
Lathi	Bamboo stave tipped with iron used By police and chowkidars
Mahajan	money lender
Maidan	parkland or greassed open space
Masala	mixture of spices used to flavour food
Masala dosa	folded pancake with spiced veg. filling
Naan	Indian flatbread cooked in tandoor oven
Namaskar	Hindu word of greeting
Nimbu	lemon or lime
Nirvana	spiritual enlightment
Paan	folded leaf with spiced Araca nut or other fillings, including tobacco, a stimulant
Pandit (Pundit)	Hindu scholar
Pani	water
Paratha	Indian flatbread fried in ghee
Patti	sub division of a market
Puja	religious devotions
Pukka	good, sound, correct
Puri	small puffed breads fried in ghee
Rickshaw	hand pulled, wheeled small carriage
Roti	Indian bread
Sabzi	vegetable
Sadhu	Hindu holy man
Sag	spinach
Sambhar	masala lentil sauce
Sardar	chief, boss, leader
Salwar kameez	women's costume of long blouse and loose trousers
Sati	now outlawed tradition of widow burning
Sepoy	Indian foot soldier

Shaan wallah	knife grinder
Shishi bottle wallah	scavenger of plastic bottles
Shri	respectful prefix to name
Tank	artificial water reservoir
Tempo	large 3 wheeled motorised vehicle
Thali	veg. or non veg. set lunch meal
Tiffin	light snack or luncheon
Tilak	Hindu sacred forehead mark
Tonga	light 2 wheeled horse drawn carriage (now rarely seen)
Untouchables	the 'scheduled' or lowest castes
Upanishads	Hindu scriptures
Vaishya	traditional trading caste
Wallah	man e.g. dhobi wallah = laundry man
Wojon wallah	man in the street with bathroom scales on which you can weigh yourself for a fee.
Yogi	Hindu ascetic
Zamindar	major landlord
Zarda	a form of cut tobacco often mixed in paan
Zindabad	lit. 'long live' much used at political rallies

Old and New Street Names

Old Name	New Name
Amherst Street	Raja Rammohan Sarani
Arpuli Lane	Surendralal Pyne Lane
Auckland Road	Sahid Khudiram Bose Road
Baitakkhanna 1st Lane	Debendra Nath Roy Lane
Banamali Sarkar Street	Gopeswar Pal Street
Bancharam Arkur Lane	Dhiren Dhar Sarani
Banerjee Bagan Lane	Banerjee Bagan Road
Banstala Street	Sir Hariram Goenka Street
Basak Dighi Lane	Kedar Banerjee Lane
Basak Lane	Gurudas Basak Lane
Beadon Street (part)	Ahbedandra Road
Beadon Street (part)	Dani Ghosh Sarani
Beadon Square	Rabindra Kanan
Belgachia Road	Khudiram Bose Sarani
Beliaghata Main Road	Dr Suresh Ch. Benerji Road
Beniapukur Road	Hare Krishna Konar Road
Biren Roy Road	Raja Rammohan Road
Blacquire Square	Sadhak Ramprasad Udyan
Bosepara Lane (part)	Ma Saradamoni Lane
Bowbazar Street	B.B. Ganguly Street
Bowpara Lane	Gopi Sen Lane
Brabourne Road	Biplabi Trailokya Maharaj Road
British Indian Street	Abdul Hamil Street
Calvert Road	Nafar Koley Road
Canning Street	Biplabi Rash Behari Bose Road
Charnock Place	Netaji Subhas Road
Charakdanga Road	Kabi Sukanta Sarani

Old Name	New Name
Chitpur Road (Upper & Lower)	Rabindra Sarani
Chitpur Bridge Approach	Mohit Moitra Sarani
Chor Bagan Lane	Amar Bose Sarani
Chowringhee (part)	Jawaharlal Nehru Road
Chutapara Lane	Harish Sikdar Path
Clive Ghat Street	Narendra Ch. Dutta Sarani
Clive Row	Dr Rajendra Prasad Sarani
Coolootola Street (part)	Maulana Sawkat Ali Street
Coolootola Street (part)	Anagarika Dharmapal Street
Coolootola Street (part)	Acharya Brojen Sil Street
College Square	Vidyasagar Udyan
Cornwallis Street	Bidhan Sarani
Cornwallis Square	Urquhart Square
Corris Church Lane	Dr Kartick Bose Street
Cotton Street	Utkalmoni Gopabandhu Sarani
Cross Street	Jamuna Lal Bajaj Street
Dacres Lane	James Hickey Sarani
Darga Gully	Coolootola Lane & By-Lane
Dalhousie Square	Binoy Badal Dinesh Bagh
Dihi Serampur Road	Rameswar Shaw Road
Dilkhusa Street	Dr Biresh Guha Street
Dharmatala Street	Lenin Sarani
Doyehatta Street	Digamber Jain Temple Road
Dukuria Bagan Lane	Amiya Hazra Lane
Eden Hospital Road	Dr Lalit Banerjee Sarani
European Asylum Lane	Comrade Andiul Halim Lane
Fancy Lane	Pannalal Bannerjee Lane
Free School Street	Mirza Ghalib Street
Galiff Street	MahatmaSisir Krishna Sarani
Gas Street	Dr M.N. Chatterjee Sarani
Gomesh Lane	Kabi Nabin Sen Lane
Grey Street (Extension)	Sri Arabindra Sarani
Hanuman Gully	Synagogue Street
Haritaki Bagan Lane	Dr Dhirendra Nath Sen Sarani
Harkata Lane	Nabin Chand Borel Lane

Old Name	New Name
Harrison Road	Mahatma Ghandi Road
Hastings Street	Kiron Sankar Roy Road
Hayat Khan Lane	Manindra Nath Mitra Road
Hiralal Mitra Lane	Uma Charan Mitra Lane
Holwell Lane	B. Ramnath Biswas Lane
India Exchange Place	William Carey Sarani
Jeliatola Street	Sudhir Chatterjee Street
Kankurgachi 3rd Lane	Sachin Mitra Lane
Karaya Bazar Lane	North Range
Karaya Lane	Kazi Abdul Wadud Sarani
Karbala Road	Rafi Ahmed Kidwai Road
Kentophar Lane	Satish Ch. Mukhopadhya Sarani
Koliaghata Street	B. Terapada Mukherjee Sarani
Kyd Street	Dr Md. Isak Road
Lawrance Road	Rani Rashmoni Avenue
Lindsay Street	Neli Sengupta Sarani
Lower Circular Road	Acharya J.C. Bose Road
MacCarthy Lane	Sudhir Sen Barat Lane
Maharani Hemanta Kr. Street	Gourimata Sarani
Mangoe Lane	Surendra Mohan Ghosh Sarani
Marquis Street	Mustaque Ahmed Street
Manicktala Street	Sisir Bhaduri Sarani
Marcus Square	Charlie Chaplin Square
Marsden Street	Paymental Street
Mayo Road	Guru Nanek Sarani
Mechua Bazar Street	Madan Mohan Burman Street
Mission Row	R.N. Mukherjee Road
Mirzapur Street	Surya Sen Street
Mott Lane	Monilal Saha Lane
Muktaram Road	Rajendra Deb Sarani
Narkeldanga Lane	Dr Jagabandhu Babu Lane
Nebutala-Ka-Rasta	Pollock Street

Old Name	*New Name*
Neogi Lane	Silpi Netai Pal Lane
Neogipukur Lane	Taltala Library Row
North Range	M. Roy Chowdhury Road
Nurmal Lohia Lane	Nurmal Lohia Street
Octerlony Road	Rani Rashmoni Avenue
Old Court House Street	Hemanta Bose Sarani
Pageya Putty Street	Basantial Murarka Road
Panchukhansama Lane	Dr Debendra Mukherjee Row
Pearl Road	Dr A.M.O. Ghani Road
Phul Bagan Road	Sir Sued Ahmed Road
Portuguese Church Street	Sahid Nityananda Sarani
Princep Street (part)	Biplabi Anukul Chandra Street
Rash Bagan Lane	Dr Panchanan Mitra Lane
Ripon Street	Muzaffar Ahmed Street
Sandal Street	Moulana A.R. Malinhabad St.
Sealdah Fly Over	Bidyapati Setu
Schalk Street	Durgacharan Banerjee Street
Scott Lane	Rajkumar Chakraborty Sarani
Shaikpara Lane	Ramdhan Khan Lane
Simla Street	Dr Narayan Roy Sarani
Sooterkin Street	Prafulla Sarkar Street
Soorepara	Ghosh Lane
South Road	Dr Suresh Sarkar Road
St. James Square	Santosh Mitra Square
Sukea Row	Daud Ali Dutta Sarani
Talapark Avenue	Tara Sankar Sarani
Talpukur Road	K.G. Basu Sarani
Taltala Avenue	Puran Chand Nahar Avenue
Tari Khana Gully	Raja Debendra Narayan Lane
Theatre Road	Shakespeare Sarani
Upper Circular Road	Acharya Prafulla Chandra Rd.
Wellesley Street	Rafi Ahmed Kidwai Road
Wellesley 1st Lane	Abdul Ali Row

Old Name	New Name
Wellesley 2nd Lane	A.K. Md. Siddiq Lane
Wellington Lane	Raj Kumar Bose Lane
Wellington Street	Nirmal Chandra Street
Wellington Square	Raja Subodh Mullick Square
William Lane	Dr Amal Roy Chowdhury Lane

ANNEXE 4

Index

Tara Chand Dutta Street, 44
Tarak Pramanick Road, 85
Teliapara Lane, 72, 73
Thakur Radhakanta Lane, 68
Thanthania Kalibari, 127
The Park, 27
Tiretta Bazar, 34, 42, 43
Toong On Church, 42
Trams, 6, 13, 56, 93, 161,
   177,

U

Udbodhan Lane, 67
Uma Das Lane, 149
Umichand, 107, 108, 109
Urquhart Square, 120, 121,
   228

V

Vansittart Henry, 212
Victoria Memorial, 2
Victoria Terrace, 8
Vidyasagar, 154
Vidyasagar Setu, 16, 216

Vivekananda Road, 80, 93,
   107, 110, 116, 121, 123,
   127, 203
Vivekananda Swami, 70, 110,
   121

W

Warren Hastings, 112, 170,
   171, 173, 212, 213,
Watson Admiral Charles, 189
Waverly Lane, 152
Wellesley Square, 149
Wellesley Street, 7, 148, 231
White Town, 21, 109, 181, 185
Wilson's Hotel, 23
Wojon Wallah, 127, 226
Writers' Building, 2, 27, 28 29

Y

Yhudi Market, 126

Z

Zakaria Street, 15, 44

Lightning Source UK Ltd.
Milton Keynes UK
UKOW05f1938200114

224955UK00001B/134/P